THE
MASONIC MANUAL

A POCKET COMPANION FOR THE INITIATED CONTAINING THE RITUALS OF FREEMASONRY

(1853)

Embraced in the Degrees of the Lodge, Chapter and Encampment; Embellished with Three Hundred Engravings; Together with Forms of Masonic Documents, Notes, Songs, Dates, etc. Very scarce!

Robert Macoy

ISBN 0-7661-0067-7

Kessinger Publishing, LLC
U.S.A.
http://www.kessingerpub.com

THE
MASONIC MANUAL.

A Pocket Companion for the Initiated:

CONTAINING THE

RITUALS OF FREEMASONRY,

EMBRACED IN THE DEGREES OF THE

LODGE, CHAPTER AND ENCAMPMENT;

EMBELLISHED WITH

Upwards of Three Hundred Engravings.

TOGETHER WITH

FORMS OF MASONIC DOCUMENTS, NOTES, SONGS, DATES, ETC.

COMPILED AND ARRANGED

BY ROBERT MACOY,

PAST MASTER, PAST GRAND SECRETARY, PAST GRAND COMMANDER, GRAND RECORDER, ETC.

FIFTEENTH EDITION.

New York:
CLARK & MAYNARD,
3 PARK ROW.

PRINTED BY

C. A. ALVORD, NEW YORK.

PREFACE

Though hard's our task, we fearless tread this ground,
    Hope whispers us, "No work is perfect found."
Has any mortal eye a perfect work e'er seen?
    Look not from us, for what has never been!
How can imperfect man expect to find,
    That which is not within the human mind!
That being the case, our work we humbly trust
    T' the Brother's candor—Masons will be just.

N presenting to the Fraternity another edition of the "MASONIC MANUAL," in an enlarged and more comprehensive character, the compiler cannot forego the opportunity of acknowledging his obligations to the Brotherhood, for the very liberal and flattering testimonials of their approbation extended to him, as well as to those who have taken so warm an interest in the appearance of the present edition.

The great aim of the present issue is intended to fill a VACUUM long existing in the Order—that of rendering, in a practical sense, the best method of assisting the learner in acquiring a knowledge of the rites and ceremonies of the various branches of the Order, principally through the aid of well arranged emblems, illustrating the symbols of the Craft.

Notwithstanding the symbolic character of Freemasonry being almost exclusively confined to the three primitive degrees, the compiler, desirous of aiding the studious novitiate, in his laudable ambition to climb the ladder of Masonic Preferment, has copiously embellished the chapitral degrees with many entirely new and appropriate emblems, illustrating the lectures therein, and with such perspicuity as to render a thorough understanding of them easy of attainment, while they remain an impenetrable mystery to those who have not had the advantage of initiation.

The degrees of Knighthood have also been favored with a variety of plain and intelligible designs, emblematical of those beautiful subsidiary appendages to Freemasonry, and so far rendered applicable to the work as to require but little further elucidation to familiarize the Sir Knight with the minutiæ of the chivalric branch of the institution.

The numerous representations of JEWELS, for Grand and Subordinate Lodges, Chapters and Encampments, selected from every accessible authentic source, will, no doubt, be practically beneficial to the members of the fraternity.

The Charges, Ceremonies of Consecration, Dedication and Installation, are selected from the works of the oldest standard Masonic writers, with such corrections only as are deemed essential to avoid prolixity of verbiage

The subjoined Forms of Masonic Documents are highly esteemed for their utility and correctness, and are estimated as articles of great value to the Craft generally.

The entire work has been prepared with the utmost attention to accuracy, and a due regard to the solemn injunction—" to preserve the ancient landmarks of the Order." The compiler asks but an examination of its internal arrangements, to convince the reader that no expense has been spared in furnishing a very extensive "MASONIC POCKET COMPANION," and, in presenting it to the Brotherhood, he desires that it shall stand entirely upon its merits for their approbation.

THE COMPILER.

PREFACE TO THE THIRD EDITION

THE very flattering interest manifested by the Fraternity of Free and Accepted Masons, in the prosperity of the "MASONIC MANUAL," has induced the compiler to issue another and improved edition of the work. Testimonials of its usefulness, and the benefit to be realized by its promulgation among a happy, prosperous, and rapidly increasing institution, are a sufficient incentive to continue to labor in a good cause, and are a positive approval of its good effects.

The Masonic Press throughout the country has generously passed a rigid and critical judgment upon its merits, and pronounced it as "weighed in the Masonic balance, and not found wanting."

The compiler thankfully avails himself of this opportunity of returning his sincere acknowledgments to the members of the institution, in which he is proud of being permitted to be a humble co-worker.

Many valuable corrections have been made in the work—several additions have also been deemed essential, to render the volume all that the most industrious and persevering Masonic student could require, in the execution of the arduous, yet beautiful ritual of the Order.

COMPILER.

CONTENTS.

vi CONTENTS.

INTRODUCTION

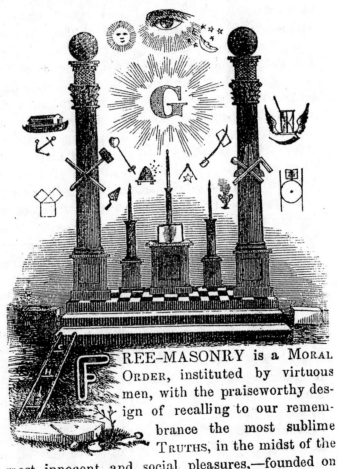

FREE-MASONRY is a MORAL ORDER, instituted by virtuous men, with the praiseworthy design of recalling to our remembrance the most sublime TRUTHS, in the midst of the most innocent and social pleasures,—founded on LIBERALITY, BROTHERLY LOVE and CHARITY. It is

a beautiful SYSTEM OF MORALITY, veiled in allegory and illustrated by symbols. TRUTH is its
centre,—the point whence its radii diverge, point
out to its disciples a correct knowledge of the Great
Architect of the Universe, and the moral laws
which he has ordained for their government.

A proper administration of the various ceremonies connected with our ritual is of the first importance and worthy of our serious consideration. The
rites and ceremonies of Free-masonry form the
distinctive peculiarity of the Institution. In their
nature they are simple—in their end instructive.
They naturally excite a high degree of curiosity
in a newly initiated brother, and create an earnest
desire to investigate their meaning, and to become
acquainted with their object and design. It requires, however, both serious application and
untiring diligence to ascertain the precise nature
of every ceremony which our ancient brethren saw
reason to adopt in the formation of an exclusive
system, which was to pass through the world un-
connected with the religion and politics of all
times, and of every people among whom it should
flourish and increase. In order to preserve our
ceremonies from the hand of innovation, it is
essentially necessary that every officer should be
thoroughly acquainted with them, and that a firm
determination should exist among the craft to admit
no change. A few words here or there may not in
themselves appear of much consequence, yet, by

frequent allowance, we become habituated to them, and thus open the door to evils of more serious magnitude. There is, there can be, no safety but in a rigid adherence to the ancient ceremonies of the Order.

The first of these that claim our attention are those employed in opening and closing the Lodge; much might here be said in relation to them did they, in our opinion, admit of written elucidation, but as they are necessarily kept within the body of the Lodge, nothing but vague and unsatisfactory hints could be given respecting them, we therefore prefer to pass them in silence, urging as a recommendation to visit each other as thebest method of keeping out innovation and preserving entire uniformity.

In connection with this ceremony, a variety of charges have, at various times, been used by the Order; from the number, we cull the two following, as well for their simple beauty as for the wholesome truths contained in them.

CHARGE AT OPENING.

"The ways of virtue are beautiful. Knowledge is attained by degrees. Wisdom dwells with contemplation: there we must seek her. Let us then, Brethren, apply ourselves with becoming zeal to the practice of the excellent principles inculcated by our Order. Let us ever remember that the great objects of our association are, the restraint of improper desires and passions, the cultivation of an active benevolence, and the promotion of a correct knowledge of the duties we owe to God, our neighbor and ourselves. Let us be united, and practise with assiduity the sacred tenets of our Order. Let all private animosities, if any unhappily exist, give place to affection and brotherly love. It is a useless parade to talk of the subjection of irregular passions within the walls of the Lodge, if we permit them to triumph in our intercourse with each other. Uniting in the grand design, let us be happy ourselves and endeavor to promote the happiness of others. Let us cultivate the great moral virtues which are laid down on our Masonic Trestleboard, and improve in every thing that is good, amiable and useful. Let the benign Genius of the Mystic Art preside over our councils, and under her sway let us act with a dignity becoming the high moral character of our venerable Institution."

CHARGE AT CLOSING

"Brethren: You are now to quit this sacred retreat of friendship and virtue, to mix again with the world. Amidst its concerns and employments, forget not the duties you have heard so frequently inculcated and forceably recommended in this Lodge. Be diligent, prudent, temperate, discreet. Remember that around this altar you have promised to befriend and relieve every Brother, who shall need your assistance. Remember that you have promised to remind him, in the most tender manner, of his failings, and aid his reformation. Vindicate his character, when wrongfully traduced. Suggest in his behalf the most candid and favorable circumstances. Is he justly reprehended ?—Let the world observe how Masons love one another.

"These generous principles are to extend further. Every human being has a claim upon your kind offices. 'Do good unto all.' Recommend it more 'especially to the household of the FAITHFUL.'

"By diligence in the duties of your respective callings; by liberal benevolence and diffusive charity; by constancy and fideiity in your friendships, discover the beneficial and happy effects of this ancient and honorable Institution. Let it not be supposed that you have here 'LABORED in vain, and spent your STRENGTH for nought; for your WORK is with the LORD and your RECOMPENSE with your GOD.'

"Finally, Brethren, be ye all of one mind,—live in peace, and may the God of love and peace delight to dwell with and bless you!"

The ancient manner prescribed for the admission of candidates also claims our attention, and we here insert it, lest in this age of new inventions any method should be found supplanting that which has for ages been the practice of the Fraternity.

ADMISSION OF CANDIDATES.

By the regulations of the Fraternity, a candidate for the mysteries of Masonry cannot be initiated in any regular Lodge, without having stood proposed one regular meeting, unless a dispensation be obtained in his favor. All applications for initiation should be made in writing, giving name, residence, age, occupation and references.

The petition, having been read in open Lodge, is placed on file. A committee is then appointed to investigate the character and qualifications of the petitioner. If, at the next regular meeting of the Lodge, the report of the Committee be favorable, and the candidate is admitted, he is required to give his free and full assent to the following interrogations:

1. "Do you seriously declare, upon your honor, before these gentlemen, that, unbiased by friends, and uninfluenced by mercenary motives, you freely and voluntarily offer yourself a candidate for the mysteries of Masonry?

2. "Do you seriously declare, upon your honor, before these gentlemen, that you are prompted to solicit the privileges of Masonry by a favorable opinion conceived of the Institution, a desire of knowledge, and a sincere wish of being serviceable to your fellow-creatures?

3. "Do you seriously declare, upon your honor, before these gentlemen, that you will cheerfully conform to all the ancient established usages and customs of the Fraternity?"

The candidate, if no objections be urged to the contrary, is then introduced in due and ancient form.

Having thus spoken of the Lodge and its officers, a few words to the craft themselves might not be deemed out of place; but we prefer to speak to them in the plain yet eloquent language of the following charges, worthy the attention of all men, and particularly the zealous enquirer for MASONIC TRUTH.

~~~~~~~~~~

ANCIENT CHARGES.

THE PRIVATE DUTIES OF MASONS.

Whoever would be a Mason should know how to practise all the private virtues. He should avoid all manner of intemperance or excess, which might prevent his performance of the laudable duties of his Craft, or lead him into enormities which would reflect dishonor upon the ancient Fraternity. He is to be industrious in his profession, and true to the Master he serves. He is to labor justly, and not to eat any man's bread for nought; but to pay truly for his meat and drink. What leisure his labor allows, he is to employ in studying the arts and sciences with a diligent mind, that he may the better perform all his duties to his Creator, his country, his neighbor and himself.

He is to seek and acquire, as far as possible, the virtues of patience, meekness, self-denial, forbearance, and the like, which give him the command over himself, and enable him to govern his own family with affection, dignity and prudence: at the same time checking every disposition injurious to the world and promoting that love and service which Brethren of the same household owe to each other.

Therefore, to afford succor to the distressed, to divide our bread with the industrious poor, and to put the misguided traveler into the way, are duties of the Craft, suitable to its dignity and expressive of its usefulness. But, though a Mason is never to shut his ear unkindly against the complaints of any of the human race, yet when a Brother is oppressed or suffers, he is in a more peculiar manner called upon to open his whole soul in love and compassion to him, and to relieve him without prejudice, according to his capacity.

It is also necessary, that all who would be true Masons should learn to abstain from all malice, slander and evil speaking; from all provoking, reproachful and ungodly language; keeping always a tongue of good report.

A Mason should know how to obey those who are set over him; however inferior they may be in worldly rank or condition. For although Masonry divests no man of his honors and titles, yet, in a Lodge, pre-eminence of virtue, and knowledge in the art, is considered as the true source of all nobility, rule and government.

The virtue indispensably requisite in Masons is—SECRECY. This is the guard of their confidence, and the security of their trust. So great a stress is to be laid upon it, that it is enforced under the strongest obligations; nor, in their esteem, is any man to be accounted wise, who has not intellectual strength and ability sufficient to cover and conceal such honest scerets as are committed to him, as well as his own more serious and private affairs.

DUTIES AS CITIZENS.

A Mason is a peaceable citizen, and is never to be concerned in plots and conspiracies against the peace and welfare of the nation, nor to behave himself undutifully to inferior magistrates. He is cheerfully to conform to every lawful authority; to uphold on every occasion, the interest of the community, and zealously promote the prosperity of his own country. Masonry has ever flourished in times of peace, and been always injured by war, bloodshed and confusion; so that kings and princes in every age, have been much disposed to encourage the craftsmen on account of their peaceableness and loyalty, whereby they practically answer the cavils of their adversaries and promote the honor of the Fraternity. Craftsmen are bound by peculiar ties to promote peace, cultivate harmony, and live in concord and Brotherly Love.

DUTIES IN THE LODGE.

While the Lodge is open for work, Masons must hold no private conversation or committees, without leave from the Master; nor talk of anything foreign or impertinent; nor interrupt the Master or Wardens, or any Brother addressing himself to the Chair; nor behave inattentively, while the Lodge is engaged in what is serious and solemn; but every Brother shall pay due reverence to the Master, the Wardens, and all his fellows.

Every Brother guilty of a fault shall submit to the Lodge, unless he appeal to the Grand Lodge.

No private offences, or disputes about nations, families, religions or politics, must be brought within the doors of the Lodge.

DUTIES AS NEIGHBORS.

Masons ought to be moral men. Consequently they should be good husbands, good parents, good sons and good neighbors; avoiding all excess, injurious to themselves or families, and wise as to all affairs, both of their own household and of the Lodge, for certain reasons known to themselves.

DUTIES TOWARDS A BROTHER.

Free and Accepted Masons have ever been charged to avoid all slander of true and faithful Brethren, and all malice or unjust resentment, or talking disrespectfully of a Brother's person or performance. Nor must they suffer any to spread unjust reproaches or calumnies against a Brother behind his back, nor to injure him in his fortune occupation or character; but they shall defend such a Brother, and give him notice of any danger or injury wherewith he may be threatened, to enable him to escape the same, as far as is consistent with honor, prudence, and the safety of religion, morality, and the state; but no farther.

ENTERED APPRENTICE
SECTION I

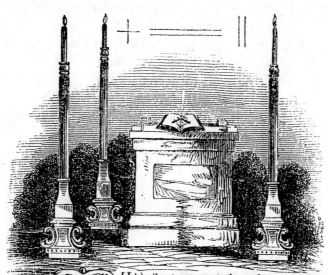

THE first step taken by a candidate, on entering a Lodge of Free masons, teaches him the pernicious tendency of infidelity, and shows him that the foundation on which Masonry rests, is the belief and acknowledgment of a Supreme being; that in Him alone a sure confidence can be safely placed to protect his steps in all the dangers and difficulties he may be called to encounter in his progress through life; it assures him that, if his faith be well founded in that Being, he may confidently pursue his course without fear and without danger

Masonry was originally an operative society, and in that form those who worked as ENTERED APPRENTICES, were styled the *first class;* but in Speculative or Free-masonry, the degree of which we are now treating is regarded as the first of the order. Its reception places the noviciate in possession of the masonic alphabet, and discloses to him the fundamental principles of this time-honored institution. It is divided into three sections, viz: 1st. The ceremony; 2d. Its moral, and 3d. Its necessity and consistency.

A full and perfect knowledge of this section is indispensably necessary to every Mason, who would be serviceable to the Institution, and would avail himself of its privileges and its enjoyments.

PRAYER USED AT THE INITIATION OF A CANDIDATE.

"Vouchsafe thine aid, Almighty father of the Universe, to this our present convention; and grant that this candidate for Masonry may dedicate and devote his life to thy service, and become a true and faithful Brother among us. Endue him with a competency of thy divine Wisdom, that by the influence of the pure principles of our Order, he may the better be enabled to display the beauties of holiness, to the honor of thy holy name. Amen

Response—"So mote it be."

THE FOLLOWING PASSAGE OF SCRIPTURE MAY BE
REHEARSED DURING THE CEREMONY.

" Behold! how good and how pleasant it is for
brethren to dwell together in unity:

" It is like the precious ointment upon the head,
that ran down upon the beard, even Aaron's beard,
that went down to the skirts of his garment:

" As the dew of Hermon, and as the dew that
descended upon the mountains of Zion: for there
the Lord commanded the blessing, even life for
evermore."

OR THE FOLLOWING ODE MAY BE SUNG:
Music—"Auld Lang Syne."

Behold! how pleasant and how good,
    For brethren such as we,
Of the " Accepted" brotherhood
    To dwell in unity!
'T is like the oil on Aaron's head
    Which to his feet distils;
Like Hermon's dew so richly shed
    On Zion's sacred hills

For there the Lord of light and love
    A blessing sent with power;
Oh, may we all this blessing prove,
    E'en life forevermore:
On Friendship's altar rising here
    Our hands now plighted be,
To live in *love* with hearts sincere.
    In *peace* and *unity*

It is the duty of the Master of the Lodge, as one of the precautionary measures of initiation, to explain to the candidate the nature and design of the Institution. And while he informs him that it is founded on the purest principles of virtue; that it possesses great and invaluable privileges, and that in order to secure those privileges to worthy men, and worthy men alone, voluntary pledges of fidelity are required. He will at the same time assure him that nothing will be expected of him incompatible with his civil, moral or religious duties.

That ancient and spotless ensign of Masonry, the LAMB-SKIN or WHITE APRON, is presented in behalf of the Lodge and the fraternity in general.

 "It is an emblem of innocence, and the badge of a Mason; more ancient than the golden fleece, or Roman eagle; more honorable than the star and garter, or any other order that can be conferred upon the candidate at the time of his initiation, or at any future period. by king, prince, potentate, or any other person, except he be a Mason." * * * It is hoped he will wear it with pleasure to himself and honor to the fraternity.

The newly initiated brother is then conducted to his proper station. * * * * * *

In the course of this section is exhibited a beautiful and impressive illustration of the first, and one of the grand principles of the institution; and concludes with a moral application of

THE WORKING TOOLS OF AN ENTERED APPRENTICE

"The *twenty-four inch gauge* is an instrument used by operative masons to measure and lay out their work; but we, as free and accepted masons, are taught to make use of it for the more noble and glorious purpose of dividing our time. It being divided into twenty-four equal parts, is emblematical of the twenty-four hours of the day, which we are taught to divide into three equal parts; whereby are found eight hours for the service of GOD, and a distressed worthy brother; eight for our usual vocations; and eight for refreshment and sleep.

"The *common gavel* is an instrument made use of by operative masons to break off the corners of rough stones, the better to fit them for the builder's use; but we, as free and accepted masons, are taught to make use of it for the more noble and

glorious purpose of divesting our hearts and consciences of all the vices and superfluities of life;
thereby fitting our minds as living stones for that
spiritual building, that house not made with hands,
eternal in the heavens."

SECTION II.

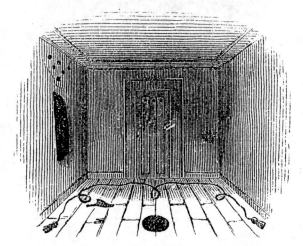

This section is one of vital importance, not only
to the candidate, but to the craft generally, and
should be properly understood by every presiding
officer; as all ceremonies would appear light and
frivolous, unless accompanied by those moral lessons and fraternal impressions which they are intended so strongly to impress on the minds of all who
pass through or witness them, that neither time nor
circumstance can eradicate them from the memory.

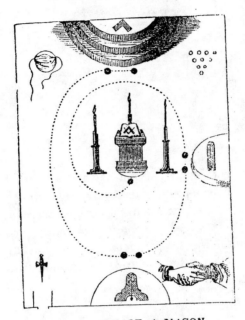

THE BADGE OF A MASON.

Every candidate, at his initiation, is presented with a *lamb-skin*, or *white apron*.

"The LAMB has, in all ages, been deemed an emblem of *innocence*; the lamb-skin is therefore to remind him of that purity of life and conduct, which is so essentially necessary to his gaining admission into the Celestial Lodge above, where the Supreme Architect of the universe presides."

SECTION III

 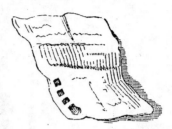

This section fully explains the manner of constituting, and the proper authority for holding a Lodge Here also, we learn where Lodges were anciently held; their *form, support, covering, furniture, ornaments, lights* and *jewels;* how situated, and to whom dedicated, as well in former times as at present.

*   *   *   *   *   *   *   *

Lodge meetings at the present day, are usually held in upper chambers—probably for the better security which such places afford. It may be, how·

ever, that the custom had its origin in a practice
observed by the ancient Jews, of building their
temples, schools and synagogues, on high hills—a
practice which seems to have met the approbation
of the Almighty, who said unto the prophet EZE-
KIEL, "upon the top of the mountain, the whole
limit thereof, round about shall be most holy."
Before the erection of temples, the *celestial* bodies
were worshipped on HILLS, and the *terrestial* ones
in VALLEYS. At a later period, the Christians,
wherever it was practicable, erected their churches
on eminences.

Its *form* is * * * *. Its dimensions from
east to west, embracing every clime between north
and south; in fact its universal chain of friendship
encircles every portion of the human family, and
beams wherever civilization extends * * * *

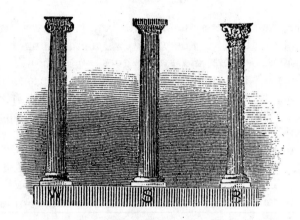

The Masonic Lodge, bounded only by the extreme points of the compass, the highest heavens, and the lowest depth of the central abyss, is metaphorically *supported* by three great pillars, which are denominated WISDOM, STRENGTH and BEAUTY; because there should be *wisdom* to contrive, *strength* to support, and *beauty* to adorn all great and important undertakings. The universe is the temple of the DEITY whom we serve; Wisdom, Strength and Beauty are about his throne as pillars of his work; for his wisdom is infinite, his strength is omnipotence, and his beauty shines forth through all his creation in symmetry and order.

TS COVERING is no less than the clouded canopy or starry-decked heaven, where all good Masons hope at last to arrive, by the aid of that theological ladder, which Jacob, in his vision, saw ascending from earth to heaven; the three *principal rounds* of which are denominated FAITH, HOPE and CHARITY; which admonish us to have *faith* in GOD, *hope* in immortality, and *charity* to all mankind. The greatest of these is CHARITY, for our *faith* may be lost in sight; *hope* ends in fruition; but *charity* extends beyond the grave, through the boundless realms of eternity."

Every well-governed lodge is furnished with the *Holy Bible*, the *Square* and the *Compasses*.

The Bible is dedicated to the service of God, because it is the inestimable gift of God to man, * * * * ; the square to the Master, because it is the proper Masonic emblem of his office; and the compasses to the craft, because, by a due attention to its use, they are taught to circumscribe their desires, and keep their passions within due bounds.*

---

* The following appropriate illustration of the * * * of masonry, may be given with beautiful effect:

"As more immediate guides for a Free-mason, the lodge is furnished with unerring rules, whereby he shall form his conduct. The book of the law is laid before him, that he may not say, through ignorance he erred; whatever the Great Architect of the world hath dictated to mankind, as the mode in which he would be served, and the path in which to tread is to obtain his approbation; whatever precepts he hath administered, and with whatever laws he hath inspired the sages of old, the same are faithfully comprised in the book of the law of masonry. That book reveals the duties which the Great Master of all exacts from us; open to every eye, comprehensible to every mind; then who shall say among us that he knoweth not the acceptable service?"

"The rule, the square, and the compasses, are emblematical of the conduct we should pursue in society. To observe punctuality in all our engagements, faithfully and religiously to discharge those important obligations, which we owe to God and our neighbor; to be upright in all our dealings; to hold the scale of justice in equal poise; to square our actions by the unerring rule of God's sacred word; to keep within compass and bounds with all mankind, particularly with a brother; to govern our expenses by our incomes; to curb our sensual appetites; to keep within bounds those unruly passions which oftentimes interfere with the enjoyments of society, and degrade both the man and the Free-mason: to recal to our minds, that in the great scale of existence, the whole family of mankind are upon a level with each other, and that the only question of preference among Free-masons should be, who is most wise, who is most good! For the time will come, and none of us know how soon, when death, the great leveller of all human greatness, will rob us of our distinctions, and bring us to a level with the dust."

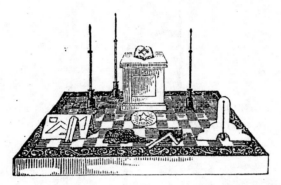

The *ornaments* of a Lodge are a representation of the *Mosaic pavement*, which formed the ground-floor of King Solomon's Temple; the beautiful *tesselated border* that surrounded it, and the *blazing star* in the centre, denoting that Masonry was originally a school of science, and that the craft have ever been solicitous to promote the same.

The *Mosaic pavement* is emblematical of human life, checkered with good and evil; the *indented tessel*, or *tesselated border*, of the manifold blessings and comforts which constantly surround us, and which we hope to enjoy by a firm reliance on Divine Providence, which is hieroglyphically represented by the *blazing star* in the centre.*

---

* 'As the steps of man are trod in the various and uncertain incidents of life; as our days are checkered with a strange contrariety of events, and our passage through this existence, though sometimes attended with prosperous circumstances, is often beset by a multitude of evils; hence is the lodge furnished with Mosaic work, to remind us of the precariousness of our state on earth; to-day, our feet tread in prosperity; to-morrow, we totter on the uneven paths of weakness, temptation and adversity. Whilst this emblem is before us, we are instructed to boast of nothing; to have compassion, and give aid to those

*   *   *   *   *   *   *   *

The *moveable* and *immoveable jewels* also claim our attention

*   *   *   *   *   *   *   *

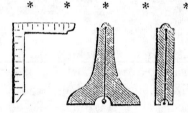

The *immoveable jewels* are the ROUGH ASHLER, the PERFECT ASHLER, and the TRESTLE BOARD.

 The *rough ashler* is a stone in its rude and natural state, as taken from the quarry: the *perfect ashler*, one prepared by the workmen, to be adjusted by the working tools of the fellow-craft ; and the *trestle board* is for the master work-man to draw his designs upon.

---

who are in adversity; to walk uprightly, and with humility; for such is this existence, that there is no station in which pride can be stably founded—all men in birth and in the grave are on a level. Whilst we tread on this Mosaic work, let our ideas return to the original which it copies; and let every mason act as the dictates of reason prompt him, to live in brotherly love."

By the *rough ashler* we are reminded of our 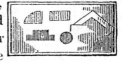 rude and imperfect state by nature; by the *perfect ashler*, of that state of perfection at which we hope to arrive by a virtuous education, our own endeavors, and the blessing of DEITY. And as the operative workman erects his temporal building in accordance with the designs laid down upon the *trestle board*, by the master workman, so should we, both operative and speculative, endeavor to erect our spiritual building in accordance with the designs laid down by the Supreme Architect of the universe, in the great book of nature and revelation, which is our spiritual, moral and masonic trestle-board.

The Lodge is situated due east and west, because King Solomon's temple was   *   *   *   *   *   *

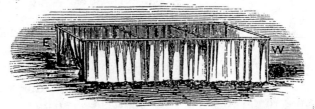

Lodges in ancient times were dedicated to King Solomon * * *, and continued to be so dedicated until after the crusades. Among the various orders of knights engaged in those chivalric wars, none were more conspicuous than the magnanimous order ot the Knights of St. John. Many brethren of our ancient craft also went forth to aid in redeeming the sepulchre of the Saviour, from the hands of the infidel; between these and the knights of St. John, there existed a reciprocal feeling of brotherly love. On the plains of Jerusalem, they entered into a solemn compact of friendship, and it was mutually agreed between them that henceforth all lodges, whose members acknowledged the divinity of Christ, should be dedicated to St. John the Baptist, and St. John the Evangelist, who were two eminent Christian patrons of Freemasonry. From that time, therefore, there has been represented, in every well-

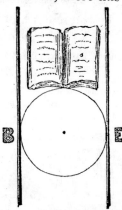

governed Lodge, a certain POINT WITHIN A CIRCLE, embordered by two perpendicular parallel lines, representing those two saints, upon the vertex of the circle rests the Holy Scriptures. The *point* within the circle represents an individual brother; the *circle* is the boundary line, beyond which he is never to suffer his passions to betray him. In going round this circle, he must necessarily touch upon these two lines, as well as the Holy Scriptures; which teaches us that while a Mason keeps himself circumscribed within their precepts, it is impossible that he should materially err.

The principal tenets of our profession are three-fold, including the inculcation and practice of those truly commendable virtues, BROTHERLY-LOVE, RE-LIEF and TRUTH

OF BROTHERLY LOVE

By the exercise of Brotherly Love, we are taught to regard the whole human species as one family; the high, the low; the rich, the poor; who, as created by one Almighty Parent and inhabitants of the same planet, are to aid, support and protect each other. On this principle, Masonry unites men of every country, sect and opinion, and conciliates true friendship among those who might otherwise have remained at a perpetual distance.

OF RELIEF

To relieve the distressed, is a duty incumbent on all men; but particularly on Masons, who are linked together by an indissoluble chain of sincere affection. To soothe the unhappy; to sympathize with their misfortunes; to compassionate their miseries, and to restore peace to their troubled minds, is the great aim we have in view. On this basis, we form our friendships and establish our connections

3

OF TRUTH.

Truth is a divine attribute, and the foundation of every virtue. To be good and true, is the first lesson we are taught in masonry. On this theme we contemplate, and by its dictates endeavor to regulate our conduct: hence, while influenced by this principle, hypocrisy and deceit are unknown among us; sincerity and plain dealing distinguish us; and the heart and tongue join in promoting each other's welfare, and rejoicing in each other's prosperity.

The Four Cardinal Virtues explained.

OF FORTITUDE.

FORTITUDE is that noble and steady purpose of the mind, whereby we are enabled to undergo any pain, peril or danger, when prudentially deemed expedient. This virtue is equally distant from rashness or cowardice; and should be deeply impressed upon the mind of every mason, as a safeguard or security against any illegal attack that may be made, by force or otherwise, to extort from him any of those valuable secrets with which he has been so solemnly intrusted, and which were emblematically represented upon his first admission into the Lodge.

*   *   *   *   *   *

OF PRUDENCE.

RUDENCE teaches us to regulate our lives and actions agreeably to the dictates of reason, and is that habit by which we wisely judge, and prudentially determine, on all things relative to our present, as well as to our future happiness. This virtue should be the peculiar characteristic of every Mason, not only for the government of his conduct while in the Lodge, but also when abroad in the world. It should be particularly attended to, in all strange and mixed companies, never to let fall the least sign, token or word, whereby the secrets of Masonry might be unlawfully obtained. * * *

OF TEMPERANCE.

EMPERANCE is that due restraint upon our affections and passions, which renders the body tame and governable, and frees the mind from the allurements of vice. This virtue should be the constant practice of every Mason; as he is thereby taught to avoid excess, or contracting any licentious or vicious habit, the indulgence of which migh' lead him to disclose some of those valuable secrets, which he has promised to conceal and never reveal, and which would consequently subject him to the contempt and detestation of all good Masons. * * * *

OF JUSTICE

USTICE is that standard, or boundary of right, which enables us to render unto every man his just due, without distinction This virtue is not only consistent with divine and human laws, but is the very cement and support of civil society; and as justice in a great measure constitutes the really good man, so should it be the invariable practice of every Mason, never to deviate from the minutest principles thereof. * * * *

The illustration of these virtues is accompanied with some general observations peculiar to Masons. Due veneration is also paid to our ancient patrons.

* * * * *

The earth is that alone of all the elements that has never proved unfriendly to man; the bodies of water deluge him with rain; oppress him with hail, and drown him with inundations. The air rushes in storms, prepares the tempest, and lights up the volcano; but the earth, ever kind and indulgent, is found subservient to his wishes; though constantly harassed, more to furnish the luxuries than the necessities of life, she never refuses her accustomed yield; spreading his path with flowers, and his table with plenty; though she produces poison, still she supplies the antidote, and returns, with interest, every good committed to her care; and when at last he is called upon to pass through the "dark valley of the shadow of Death," she once more receives him, and piously covers his remains within her bosom; this admonishes us that from it we came and to it we must shortly return.

Such is the arrangement of the different sections in the first lecture, which, with the forms adopted at the opening and closing of a Lodge, comprehends the whole of the first degree of Masonry. This plan has the advantage of regularity to recommend it, the support of precedent and authority, and the sanction and respect which flow from antiquity.

CHARGE TO THE CANDIDATE

BROTHER:—As you are now introduced into the first principles of Masonry, I congratulate you on being accepted into this ancient and honorable order:—ancient, as having subsisted from time immemorial, and honorable, as tending, in every particular, so to render all men who will be conformable to its precepts. No institution was ever

raised on a better principle, or more solid foundation; nor were ever more excellent rules and useful
maxims laid down, than are inculcated in the several Masonic lectures. The greatest and best of
men, in all ages, have been encouragers and pro-
moters of the art; and have never deemed it
derogatory to their dignity, to level themselves
with the fraternity, extend their privileges, and
patronize their assemblies. There are three great
duties, which, as a Mason, you are charged to
inculcate—to GOD, your neighbor, and yourself.
To GOD, in never mentioning his name, but with
that reverential awe which is due from a creature
to his CREATOR; to implore his aid in all your
laudable undertakings, and to esteem him as the
chief good;—to your neighbor, in acting upon the
square, and doing unto him as you wish he should
do unto you; and to yourself, in avoiding all
irregularity and intemperance, which may impair
your faculties, or debase the dignity of your profession. A zealous attachment to these duties, will
insure public and private esteem.

In the state, you are to be a quiet and peaceful
citizen, true to your government, and just to your
country; you are not to countenance disloyalty or
rebellion, but patiently submit to legal authority,
and conform with cheerfulness to the government
of the country in which you live. In your outward
demeanor, be particularly careful to avoid censure
and reproach

Although your frequent appearance at our regular meetings is earnestly solicited, yet it is not meant that masonry should interfere with your necessary vocations; for these are on no account to be neglected; neither are you to suffer your zeal for the institution to lead you into argument with those who, through ignorance, may ridicule it.

At your leisure hours, that you may improve in masonic knowledge, you are to converse with well-informed brethren, who will be always as ready to give, as you will be to receive, instruction.

Finally, keep sacred and inviolable the mysteries of the order; as these are to distinguish you from the rest of the community, and mark your consequence among masons. If, in the circle of your acquaintance, you find a person desirous of being initiated into masonry, be particularly careful not to recommend him, unless you are convinced he will conform to our rules; that the honor, glory and reputation of the institution, may be firmly established, and the world at large convinced of its good effects.

FELLOW CRAFT.

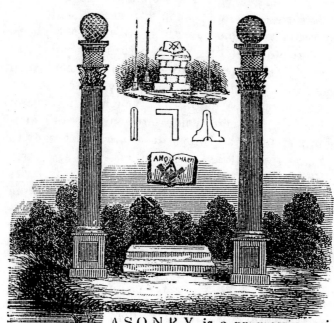

ASONRY is a progressive science, and is divided into different
classes, or degrees, for the more
regular advancement in the knowledge of its mysteries. According
to the progress we make, we limit or extend our
inquiries; and, in proportion to our capacity, we
attain to a less or greater degree of perfection.

Masonry includes within its circle almost every
branch of polite learning Under the veil of its

mysteries is comprehended a regular system of science. Many of its illustrations, to the confined genius, may appear unimportant; but the man of more enlarged faculties will perceive them to be, in the highest degree, useful and interesting. To please the accomplished scholar, and ingenious artist, Masonry is wisely planned; and, in the investigation of its latent doctrines, the philosopher and mathematician may experience equal delight and satisfaction.

To exhaust the various subjects of which it treats, would transcend the powers of the brightest genius; still, however, nearer approaches to perfection may be made; and the man of wisdom will not check the progress of his abilities, though the task he attempts may at first seem insurmountable. Perseverance and application remove each difficulty as it occurs; every step he advances new pleasures open to his view, and instruction of the noblest kind attends his researches. In the diligent pursuit of knowledge, the intellectual faculties are employed in promoting the glory of GOD, and the good of man.

The first degree is well calculated to enforce the duties of morality, and imprint on the memory the noblest principles which can adorn the human mind. It is therefore the best introduction to the second degree, which not only extends the same plan, but comprehends a more diffusive system of knowledge. Here, practice and theory join, in qualifying the industrious Mason to share the pleasures which an advancement in the art must necessarily afford. Listening with attention to the wise opinions of experienced craftsmen, on important subjects, he gradually familiarizes his mind to useful instruction, and is soon enabled to investigate truths of the utmost concern in the general transactions of life.

From this system proceeds a rational amusement; while the mental powers are fully employed, the judgment is properly exercised; a spirit of emulation prevails; and all are induced to contend, who shall most excel in promoting the valuable rules of the institution

SECTION I.

The first section of the second degree accurately elucidates the mode of introduction into that particular class; and instructs the diligent craftsman how to proceed in the proper arrangement of the ceremonies used on the occasion. It qualifies him to judge of their importance, and convinces him of the necessity of strictly adhering to every established usage of the order Here he is entrusted with particular tests, to enable him to prove his title to the privileges of this degree, while satisfactory reasons are given for their origin. Many duties, which cement in the firmest union well-informed brethren, are illustrated in this section; and an opportunity is given to make such advances in masonry, as will always distinguish the abilities of those who have arrived at preferment.

The knowledge of this section is absolutely necessary for all craftsmen; and as it recapitulates the ceremony of initiation, and contains many other important particulars, no officer or member of a lodge should be unacquainted with it.

The following passage of Scripture is appropriate to this degree:

"Thus he shewed me: and behold, the LORD stood upon a wall made by a plumb-line, with a plumb-line in his hand. And the LORD said unto me, AMOS, what seest thou? and I said, A plumb-line. Then said the LORD, Behold, I will set a plumb-line in the midst of my people Israel: I will not again pass by them any more."—AMOS, vii. 7, 8

OR THE FOLLOWING ODE MAY BE SUNG:

Come, Craftsmen, assembled our pleasure to share,
Who walk by the PLUMB, and who work by the
    SQUARE;
While traveling in love, on the LEVEL of time,
Sweet hope shall light on to a far better clime.

We'll seek, in our labors, the Spirit Divine,
Our temple to bless, and our hearts to refine;
And thus to our altar a tribute we'll bring,
While, joined in true friendship, our anthem we sing

See Order and Beauty rise gently to view,
Each Brother a column, so perfect and true !
When Order shall cease, and when temples decay,
May each, fairer columns, immortal, survey

     *   *   *   *   *   *   *   *

    The three ρ ρ ρ allude to the three * * *,
which are the * * *

    The PLUMB, SQUARE, and LEVEL, those noble
and useful implements of a Fellow Craft, are here
introduced and moralized.

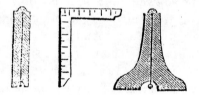

    The *Plumb*, is an instrument made use of by
operative masons, to try perpendiculars ; the *Square*,
to square their work, and the *Level*, to prove hori-
zontals ; but we, as free and accepted Masons, are
taught to make use of them for more noble and
glorious purposes ; the *Plumb* admonishes us to
walk uprightly in our several stations before GOD
and man, squaring our actions by the *Square* of
Virtue, and ever remembering that we are traveling upon the *Level* of Time, to " that undiscovered
country, from whose bourne no traveler returns."

SECTION II.

The second section of this degree has recourse to
the origin of the institution, and views Masonry
under two denominations—operative and speculative. These are separately considered, and the
principles on which both are founded, particularly
explained. Their affinity is pointed out, by allegorical figures and typical representations. The
period stipulated for rewarding merit is fixed, and
the inimitable moral to which that circumstance
alludes is explained ; the creation of the world is
described, and many other particulars recited, all
of which have been carefully preserved among
Masons, and transmitted from one age to another
by oral tradition.

Circumstances of great importance to the fraternity are here particularized, and many tradi-
tional tenets and customs confirmed by sacred and
profane record. The celestial and terrestrial
globes are considered with a minute accuracy ; and
here the accomplished craftsman may display his
talents to advantage, in the elucidation of the
Orders of Architecture, the *Senses* of human
nature, and the liberal *Arts* and *Sciences*, which
are severally classed in a regular arrangement. In
short, this section contains a store of valuable
knowledge, founded on reason and sacred record,
both entertaining and instructive.

Masonry is understood under two denominations, operative and speculative.

OPERATIVE MASONRY.

By Operative Masonry we allude to a proper application of the useful rules of architecture, whence a structure will derive figure, strength and beauty, and whence will result a due proportion and a just correspondence in all its parts. It furnishes us with dwellings, and convenient shelters from the vicissitudes and inclemencies of seasons; and while it displays the effects of human wisdom, as well in the choice as in the arrangement of the sundry materials of which an edifice is composed, it demonstrates that a fund of science and industry is implanted in man, for the best, most salutary and benificent purposes.

SPECULATIVE MASONRY.

By Speculative Masonry, we learn to subdue the passions, act upon the square, keep a tongue of good report, maintain secrecy, and practise charity. It is so far interwoven with religion, as to lay us under obligations to pay that rational homage to the DEITY, which at once constitutes our duty and our happiness. It leads the contemplative to view, with reverence and admiration, the glorious works of creation, and inspires him with the most exalted ideas of the perfection of his divine Creator

In six days GOD created the heavens and the earth,
and rested upon the seventh day; the seventh,
therefore, our ancient brethren consecrated as a day
of rest from their labors, thereby enjoying frequent
opportunities to contemplate the glorious works of
the creation, and to adore their great CREATOR.

*   *   *   *   *   *

PEACE, UNITY AND PLENTY, are introduced and their moral application explained.

The doctrine of the SPHERES is included in the science of astronomy, and particularly considered in this section.

OF THE GLOBES.

The *globes* are two artificial spherical bodies, on the convex surface of which are represented the countries, seas, and various parts of the earth, the face of the heavens, the planetary revolutions, and other important particulars.

THE USE OF THE GLOBES.

Their principal use, besides serving as maps to distinguish the outward parts of the earth, and the situation of the fixed stars, is to illustrate and explain the phenomena arising from the annual revolution, and the diurnal rotation of the earth round its own axis. They are invaluable instruments for improving the mind, and giving it the most distinct idea of any problem or proposition, as well as enabling it to solve the same. Contemplating these bodies, we are inspired with a due reverence for the DEITY and his works, and are induced to encourage the studies of astronomy, geography, navigation, and the arts dependent on them, by which society has been so much benefited

THE ORDERS OF ARCHITECTURE

Come under consideration in this section; a brief description of them may not be improper.

OF ORDER IN ARCHITECTURE

By order in architecture, is meant a system of all the members, proportions and ornaments of columns and pilasters; or, it is a regular arrangement of the projecting parts of a building, which, united with those of a column, form a beautiful, perfect and complete whole.

OF ITS ANTIQUITY

From the first formation of society, order in architecture may be traced. When the rigor of seasons obliged men to contrive shelter from the inclemency of the weather, we learn that they first planted trees on end, and then laid others across, to support a covering. The bands which connected those trees at top and bottom, are said to have given rise to the idea of the base and capital of pillars; and, from this simple hint, originally proceeded the more improved art of architecture.

The five orders are thus classed: the TUSCAN, DORIC, IONIC, CORINTHIAN AND COMPOSITE.

THE TUSCAN

Is the most simple and solid of the five orders. It was invented in Tuscany, whence it derives its name. Its column is seven diameters high; and its capital, base and entablature have but few mouldings. The simplicity of the construction of this column renders it eligible where ornament would be superfluous.

THE DORIC,

Which is plain and natural, is the most ancient, and was invented by the Greeks Its column is eight diameters high, and ha seldom any ornaments on base or capital except mouldings; though the frieze is dis tinguished by triglyphs and metopes, an triglyphs compose the ornaments of th frieze. The solid composition of this order give it a preference, in structures where strength and noble simplicity are chiefly required. The Dori is the best proportioned of all the orders. Th several parts of which it is composed are founde on the natural position of solid bodies. In its firs invention it was more simple than in its presen state. In after times, when it began to be adorned it gained the name of Doric; for when it was cor structed in its primitive and simple form, the name of Tuscan was conferred on it. Hence the Tuscan precedes the Doric in rank, on account of its resemblance to that pillar in its original state.

THE IONIC

Bears a kind of mean proportion between the more solid and delicate orders. Its column is nine diameters high; its capital is adorned with volutes, and its cornice has dentils. There is both delicacy and ingenuity displayed in this pillar; the invention of which is attributed to the Ionians, as the famous temple of DIANA, at Ephesus, was of this order. It is said to have been formed after the model of an agreeable young woman, of an elegant shape, dressed in her hair; as a contrast to the Doric order, which was formed after that of a strong, robust man.

THE CORINTHIAN,

The richest of the five orders, is deemed a master-piece of art. Its column is ten diameters high, and its capital is adorned with two rows of leaves, and eight volutes, which sustain the abacus. The frieze is ornamented with curious devices, the cornice with dentils and modillions. This order is used in stately and superb structures

It was invented at Corinth, by CALLIMACHUS, who is said to have taken the hint of the capital of this pillar from the following remarkable circumstance. Accidentally passing by the tomb of a young lady, he perceived a basket of toys, covered with a tile, placed over an acanthus root, having been left there by her nurse. As the branches grew up, they encompassed the basket, until arriving at the tile, they met with an obstruction, and bent downwards. Callimachus, struck with the object, set about imitating the figure; the vase of the capital he made to represent the basket; the abacus the tile, and the volutes the bending leaves.

THE COMPOSITE

Is compounded of the other orders, and was contrived by the Romans. Its capital has the two rows of leaves of the Corinthian and the volutes of the Ionic. It column has quarter-rounds, as the Tuscan and Doric order; is ten diameters high, and its cornice has dentils, or simple modillions. This pillar is generally found in buildings where strength, elegance and beauty are displayed.

OF THE INVENTION OF ORDER IN ARCHITECTURE.

The ancient and original orders of architecture, revered by Masons, are no more than three, the *Doric, Ionic* and *Corinthian*, which were invented by the Greeks. To these, the Romans have added two, the Tuscan, which they made plainer than the Doric, and the Composite, which was more ornamental, if not more beautiful, than the Corinthian. The first three orders alone, however, show invention and particular character, and essentially differ from each other; the two others have nothing but what is borrowed, and differ only accidentally; the Tuscan is the Doric in its earliest state; and the Composite is the Corinthian enriched with the Ionic. To the Greeks, therefore, and not to the Romans, we are indebted for what is great, judicious and distinct in architecture.

OF THE FIVE SENSES OF HUMAN NATURE.

An analysis of the human faculties is next given in this section, in which the five external senses particularly claim attention.

The senses we are to consider as the gifts of nature, and though not the acquisition of our reasoning faculty, yet in the use of them, are still subject to reason. Reason, properly employed, confirms the documents of nature, which are always true and wholesome; she distinguishes the good from the bad; rejects the last with modesty, adheres to the first with reverence. The objects of human knowledge are innumerable; the channels by which this knowledge is conveyed are few. Among these, the perception of external things by the senses, and the information we receive from human testimony, are not the least considerable;

the analogy between them is obvious. In the testimony of nature, given by the senses, as well as in human testimony, given by information, things are signified by signs. In one as well as the other, the mind, either by original principles or by custom, passes from the sign to the conception and belief of the thing signified. The signs in the natural language, as well as the signs in our original perceptions, have the same signification in all climates and nations, and the skill of interpreting them is not acquired, but innate

Having made these observations, we shall proceed to give a brief description of the five senses.

HEARING

Is that sense by which we distinguish sounds, and are capable of enjoying all the agreeable charms of music. By it we are enabled to enjoy the pleasures of society, and reciprocally to communicate to each other our thoughts and intentions, our purposes and desires; and thus our reason is rendered capable of exerting its utmost power and energy. The wise and beneficent Author of Nature, intended, by the formation of this sense, that we should be social creatures, and receive the greatest and most important part of our knowledge from social intercourse with each other. For these purposes we are endowed with hearing, that by a proper exertion of our rational powers, our happiness may be complete

SEEING

is that sense by which we distinguish objects, and
in an instant of time, without change of place
or situation, view armies in battle array, figures of
the most stately structures, and all the agreeable
variety displayed in the landscape of nature. By
this sense we find our way on the pathless ocean,
traverse the globe of earth, determine its figure
and dimensions, and delineate any region or quar-
ter of it. By it we measure the planetary orbs,
and make new discoveries in the sphere of the fixed
stars. Nay, more, by it we perceive the tempers
and dispositions, the passions and affections of our
fellow creatures, when they wish most to conceal
them ; so that, though the tongue may be taught
to lie and dissemble, the countenance will display
the hypocrisy to the discerning eye In fine, the
rays of light which administer to this sense, are
the most astonishing parts of the animated creation, and render the eye a peculiar object of
admiration.

Of all the faculties, SIGHT is the noblest. The
structure of the eye, and its appurtenances, evince
the admirable contrivance of nature for performing
all its various external and internal motions ;
while the variety displayed in the eyes of different
animals, suited to their several ways of life, clearly
demonstrates this organ to be the master-piece of
nature's works

FEELING

Is that sense by which we distinguish the different qualities of bodies; such as heat and cold, hardness and softness, roughness and smoothness, figure, solidity, motion and extension.

These three senses, *hearing*, *seeing*, and *feeling*, are deemed peculiarly essential among masons.

*　　*　　*　　*　　*　　*　　*　　*

SMELLING

Is that sense by which we distinguish odors, the various kinds of which convey different impressions to the mind. Animal and vegetable bodies, and indeed most other bodies, while exposed to the air, continually send forth effluvia of vast subtilty, as well in a state of life and growth, as in the state of fermentation and putrefaction. These effluvia, being drawn into the nostrils along with the air, are the means by which all bodies are distinguished. Hence it is evident, that there is a manifest appearance of design in the great Creator's having planted the organ of smell in the inside of that canal, through which the air continually passes in respiration

TASTING

Enables us to make a proper distinction in the choice of our food. The organ of this sense guards the entrance of the alimentary canal, as that of smelling guards the entrance of the canal for res·

piration.   From the situation of both these organs,
it is plain that they were intended by nature
to distinguish wholesome food from that which is
nauseous.   Every thing that enters into the stom-
ach must undergo the scrutiny of tasting ; and by
it we are capable of discerning the changes which
the same body undergoes in the different composi-
tions of art, cookery, chemistry, pharmacy, &c.

Smelling and tasting are inseparately connected,
and it is by the unnatural kind of life men commonly
lead in society, that these senses are rendered less
fit to perform their natural offices.

The proper use of these five senses enables us to
form just and accurate notions of the operations
of nature ; and when we reflect on the objects with
which our senses are gratified, we become conscious
of them, and are enabled to attend to them, till
they become familiar objects of thought.

On the mind all our knowledge must depend ;
what, therefore, can be a more proper subject for
the investigation of Masons ?

To sum up the whole of this transcendent
measure of GOD'S bounty to man, we shall add,
that memory, imagination, taste, reasoning, moral
perception, and all the active powers of the soul,
present a vast and boundless field for philosophical
disquisition, which far exceeds human enquiry, and
are peculiar mysteries, known only to nature, and
to nature's God, to whom all are indebted for creation, reservation, and every blessing we enjoy

THE SEVEN LIBERAL ARTS AND SCIENCES

Are also illustrated in this section. A brief anal·
ysis of the character of each, may not, therefore,
be inappropriate in this place.

GRAMMAR

Is the key by which alone the door can be opened
to the understanding of speech. It is Grammar
which reveals the admirable art of language, and
unfolds its various constituent parts, its names,
definitions, and respective offices; it unravels, as it
were, the thread of which the web of speech is
composed. These reflections seldom occur to any
one before their acquaintance with the art; yet it
is most certain, that, without a knowledge of
Grammar, it is very difficult to speak with propriety, precision, and purity.

RHETORIC.

It is by Rhetoric that the art of speaking elo-
quently is acquired. To be an eloquent speaker,
in the proper sense of the word, is far from being
either a common or an easy attainment: it is the
art of being persuasive and commanding; the art,
not only of pleasing the fancy, but of speaking
both to the understanding and to the heart

LOGIC

Is that science which directs us how to form clear
and distinct ideas of things, and thereby prevents
us from being misled by their similitude or resem-

blance. Of all the human sciences, that concerning man is certainly most worthy of the human mind, and the proper manner of conducting its several powers in the attainment of truth and knowledge. This science ought to be cultivated as the foundation or ground-work of our inquiries; particularly, in the pursuit of those sublime principles which claim our attention as masons

ARITHMETIC

Is the art of numbering, or that part of the mathematics which considers the properties of numbers in general. We have but a very imperfect idea of things without quantity, and as imperfect of quantity itself, without the help of Arithmetic. All the works of the Almighty are made in number, weight and measure; therefore, to understand them rightly, we ought to understand arithmetical calculations, and the greater advancement we make in the mathematical sciences, the more capable we shall be of considering such things as are the ordinary objects of our conceptions, and be thereby led to a more comprehensive knowledge of our great Creator, and the works of the creation.

GEOMETRY

Treats of the powers and properties of magnitudes in general, where length, breadth and thickness are considered—from a *point* to a *line*, from a line to a *superfices*, and from a superfices to a *solid*

A *point* is the beginning of all geometrical matter

A *line* is a continuation of the same.

A *superfices* is length and breadth without a given thickness.

A *solid* is length and breadth, with a given thickness, which forms a cube and comprehends th whole.

OF THE ADVANTAGES OF GEOMETRY.

By this science the architect is enabled to construct his plans, and execute his designs; the general, to arrange his soldiers; the engineer, to mark out grounds for encampments; the geographer, to give us the dimensions of the world, and all things therein contained; to delineate the extent of seas, and specify the divisions of empires, kingdoms and provinces. By it, also, the astronomer is enabled to make his observations, and to fix the duration of times and seasons, years and cycles. In fine, Geometry is the foundation of architecture, and the root of the mathematics.

MUSIC

Is that elevated science which affects the passions by sound. There are few who have not felt its charms, and acknowledged its expressions to be intelligible to the heart. It is a language of delightful sensations, far more eloquent than words; it breathes to the ear the clearest intimations; it touches and gently agitates the agreeable and sublime passions; it wraps us in melancholy, and elevates us in joy; it dissolves and enflames; it melts us in tenderness, and excites us to war. This science is truly congenial to the nature of man; for by its powerful charms, the most discordant passions may be harmonized and brought into perfect unison: but it never sounds with such seraphic harmony, as when employed in singing hymns of gratitude to the Creator of the universe.

ASTRONOMY

Is that sublime science which inspires the contemplative mind to soar aloft, and read the wisdom, strength, and beauty of the great Creator in the heavens. How nobly eloquent of the Deity is the celestial hemisphere! — spangled with the most magnificent heralds of his infinite glory! They speak to the whole universe; for there is no speech so barbarous, but their language is understood; nor nation so distant, but their voices are heard among them.

The heavens proclaim the glory of GOD;
The firmament declareth the works of his hands.

Assisted by Astronomy, we ascertain the laws which govern the heavenly bodies, and by which their motions are directed; investigate the power by which they circulate in their orbs, discover their size, determine their distance, explain their various phenomena, and correct the fallacy of the senses by the light of truth

Here an emblem of PLENTY is introduced and explained.   *   *   *   *   *

CORN.   WINE.   OIL.
     *   *   *   *   *

* * * * * * * * *

OF THE MORAL ADVANTAGES OF GEOMETRY

Geometry, the first and noblest of sciences, is the basis on which the superstructure of Free-masonry is erected. By Geometry we may curiously trace nature through her various windings, to her most concealed recesses. By it, we discover the power, wisdom and goodness of the GRAND ARTIFICER of the universe, and view with delight the proportions which connect this vast machine. By it, we discover how the planets move in their respective orbits, and demonstrate their various revolutions. By it we account for the return of the seasons, and the variety of scenes which each season displays to the discerning eye. Numberless worlds are around us, all framed by the same Divine Artist, which roll through the vast expanse, and are all conducted by the same unerring law of nature.

A survey of nature, and the observation of her beautiful proportions, first determined man to imitate the divine plan, and study symmetry and order. This gave rise to societies, and birth to every useful art. The architect began to design ; and the plans which he laid down, being improved by time and experience, have produced works which are the admiration of every age.

The lapse of time, the ruthless hand of ignorance, and the devastations of war, have laid waste and destroyed many valuable monuments of antiquity, on which the utmost exertions of human genius have been employed. Even the Temple of Solomon, so spacious and magnificent, and constructed by so many celebrated artists, escaped not the unsparing ravages of barbarous force. Freemasonry, notwithstanding, has still survived. The *attentive ear* receives the sound from the *instructive tongue*, and the mysteries of masonry are safely lodged in the repository of *faithful breasts*. Tools and implements of architecture, and symbolic emblems, most expressive, are selected by the fraternity, to imprint on the mind wise and serious truths ; and thus, through a succession of ages, are transmitted unimpaired the most excellent tenets of our institution.

*   *   *   *   *   *

Thus end the two sections of the second lecture. which, with the ceremony used at opening and closing the lodge, comprehend the whole of the second degree of masonry. This lecture contains a regular system of science, demonstrated on the clearest principles, and founded on the most stable foundation.

~~~~~~~~~~

CHARGE TO THE CANDIDATE.

BROTHER :—Being advanced to the second degree of Free-masonry, we congratulate you on your preferment. The internal, and not the external qualifications of a man, are what masonry regards As you increase in knowledge, you will improve in social intercourse.

It is unnecessary to recapitulate the duties which, as a Fellow Craft, you are bound to discharge, or to enlarge on the necessity of a strict adherence to them, as your own experience must have established their value. Our laws and regulations you are strenuously to support; and be always ready to assist in seeing them duly executed. You are not to palliate, or aggravate, the offences of your brethren; but in the decision of every trespass against our rules. you are to judge with candor, admonish with friendship, and reprehend with justice.

The study of the liberal arts, that valuable branch of education, which tends so effectually to polish and adorn the mind, is earnestly recommended to your consideration; especially the science of Geometry, which is established as the basis of our art. Geometry, or Masonry, originally synonymous terms, being of a divine and moral nature, is enriched with the most useful knowledge; while it proves the wonderful properties of nature, it demonstrates the more important truths of morality.

Your past behavior and regular deportment have merited the honor which we have now conferred; and in your new character, it is expected that you will conform to the principles of the order, by steadily persevering in the practice of every commendable virtue. Such is the nature of your engagements as a Fellow Craft, and to these duties you are bound by the most sacred ties.

MASTER MASON.

REE-MASONRY in every degree, as before remarked, is progressive. A knowledge of it can only be attained by time, patience and application. In the first degree, we are taught the duties we owe to God, our neighbor and ourselves. In the second, we are more thoroughly inducted into the mysteries of moral science, and learn to trace the goodness and majesty of the Creator, by minutely analyzing his works. But the third degree is the cement of the whole. It is calculated to bind men together by mystic points of fellowship, as in a bond of fraternal affection and Brotherly Love. It is among brethren of this degree, that the ancient landmarks of the order are preserved, and it is from them that we derive that fund of information which none but ingenious and expert masons can supply.

It is also from brethren of this degree, that the rulers of the Craft are selected; because it is only from those who are capable of giving instruction, that we can reasonably expect to receive it.

SECTION I

The first section in this, as in the two preceding degrees, is initiatory; and a knowledge of it is indispensable to every brother who would make himself useful in the ceremonial transactions of a lodge.

The following passage of Scripture is introduced during the ceremonies:

"Remember now thy Creator in the days of thy youth, while the evil days come not, nor the years draw nigh, when thou shalt say, I have no pleasure in them; while the sun, or the light, or the moon, or the stars, be not darkened, nor the clouds return after the rain: in the day when the keepers of the house shall tremble, and the strong men shall bow themselves, and the grinders cease because they

are few, and those that look out of the windows be
darkened, and the doors shall be shut in the streets,
when the sound of the grinding is low, and he shall
rise up at the voice of the bird, and all the daughters of music shall be brought low ; also, when
they shall be afraid of that which is high, and
fears shall be in the way, and the almond-tree shall
flourish, and the grasshopper shall be a burden,
and desire shall fail ; because man goeth to his long
home, and the mourners go about the streets: or
ever the silver cord be loosed, or the golden bowl be
broken, or the pitcher be broken at the fountain, or
the wheel broken at the cistern. Then shall the
dust return to the earth as it was ; and the spirit
shall return unto GOD who gave it."

OR THE FOLLOWING ODE MAY BE SUNG:

Music—" Bonny Doon."

LET us remember in our youth,
  Before the evil days draw nigh,
Our GREAT CREATOR, and his TRUTH!
  Ere memory fail, and pleasure fly ;
Or sun, or moon, or planet's light
  Grow dark, or clouds return in gloom :
Ere vital spark no more incite ;
  When strength shall bow, and years consume

Let us in youth remember HIM !
  Who formed our frame, and spirits gave,
Ere windows of the mind grow dim,
  Or door of speech obstructed wave :

When voice of bird fresh terrors wake ;
   And Music's daughters charm no more,
Or fear to rise, with trembling shake
   Along the path we travel o'er.

In youth, to GOD, let memory cling,
   Before desire shall fail, or wane,
Or e'er be loosed life's silver string,
   Or bowl at fountain rent in twain :
For man to his long home doth go,
   And mourners group around his urn ;
Our dust, to dust again must flow,
   And spirits unto GOD return

All the implements in masonry, indiscriminately, properly belong to brethren of this degree, and may be illustrated in this section. The TROWEL, however, is more particularly referred to

THE TROWEL

Is an instrument made use of by operative masons, to spread the cement which unites the building into one common mass ; but we, as free and accepted masons, are taught to make use it for the more noble and glorious purpose of spreading the cement of Brotherly Love and affection ; that cement which unites us into one sacred band, or society of friends and brothers, among whom no contention should ever exist, but that noble contention, or rather emulation. of who best can work and best agree

SECTION II.

This section recites the historical traditions of the Order, and presents to view a picture of great moral sublimity. It exemplifies an instance of virtue and firmness, seldom equaled, and never excelled.

*   *   *   *   *   *   *   *

Funeral Dirge.

Music—"Pleyel."

Solemn strikes the fun'ral chime,
Notes of our departing time ;
As we journey here below,
Through a pilgrimage of wo !

Mortals, now indulge a tear,
For mortality is near !
See how wide her trophies wave
O'er the slumbers of the grave !

Here another guest we bring,—
Seraphs of celestial wing,
To our fun'ral altar come,
Waft this friend and brother home.

There, enlarged, thy soul shall see
What was veiled in mystery ;
Heavenly glories of the place
Show his Maker face to face

Lord of all ! below—above—
Fill our hearts with truth and love ;
When dissolves our earthly tie,
Take us to thy Lodge on high

The following prayer is used at the raising of
brother to the sublime degree of Master Mason :

Thou, O God ! knowest our down-setting and
our up-rising. and understandeth our thoughts afar
off Shield and defend us from the evil intentions

of our enemies, and support us under the trials and
afflictions we are destined to endure, while traveling
through this vale of tears. Man that is born of a
woman is of few days, and full of trouble. He
cometh forth as a flower, and is cut down; he fleeth
also as a shadow, and continueth not. Seeing his
days are determined, the number of his months are
with thee; thou hast appointed his bounds that he
cannot pass: turn from him that he may rest, till
he shall accomplish his day. For there is hope of
a tree, if it be cut down, that it will sprout again,
and that the tender branch thereof will not cease.
But man dieth and wasteth away; yea, man giveth
up the ghost, and where is he? As the waters fail
from the sea, and the flood decayeth and drieth up,
so man lieth down, and riseth not up till the heavens shall be no more. Yet, O Lord! have compassion on the children of thy creation; administer
them comfort in time of trouble, and save them
with an everlasting salvation. So mote it be.
Amen

*   *   *   *   *   *

It has been the practice of all ages to erect monuments to the memory of departed worth.

*   *   *   *   *   *   *   *

SECTION III.

This section illustrates certain hieroglyphical emblems and inculcates many useful and impressive moral lessons. It also details many particulars relative to the building of the Temple at Jerusalem.

This magnificent structure was founded in the fourth year of the reign of Solomon, on the second day of the month Zif, being the second month of the sacred year. It was located on Mount Moriah,

 near the place where Abraham was about to offer
up his son Isaac, and where David met and appeased
the destroying angel. Josephus informs us, that
although more than seven years were occupied in
building it, yet, during the whole term, it did not
rain in the day time, that the workmen might not
be obstructed in their labor. From sacred history
we also learn, that there was not the sound of axe,
hammer or any tool of iron, heard in the house
while it was building.

It is said to have been supported by fourteen
hundred and fifty-three columns, and two thousand

nine hundred and six pilasters, all hewn from the finest Parian marble. There were employed in its building, three Grand Masters; three thousand and three hundred Masters or Overseers of the work; eighty thousand Fellow Crafts; and seventy thousand Entered Apprentices, or bearers of burens. All these were classed and arranged in such manner, by the wisdom of Solomon, that neither envy, discord, nor confusion, was suffered to interrupt or disturb the peace and good fellowship which prevailed among the workmen

In front of the magnificent porch, were placed the two celebrated pillars,—one on the left hand and one on the right hand. They are supposed to have been placed there as a memorial to the children of Israel, of the happy deliverance of their forefathers from Egyptian bondage, and in commemoration of the miraculous pillars of fire and cloud. The pillar of fire gave light to the Israelites and facilitated their march, and the cloud proved darkness to Pharaoh and his host, and retarded their pursuit. King Solomon, therefore, ordered these pillars to be placed at the entrance of the temple, as the most conspicuous part, that the children of Israel might have that happy event continually before their eyes, in going to and returning from divine worship.

* * * * * * * *

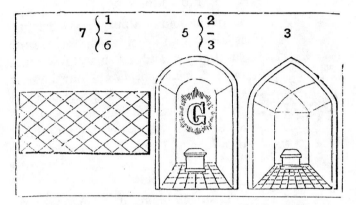

In this section are also explained a variety of appropriate emblems, with which the skilful brother will not fail to make himself familiarly acquainted. Among them are the following:

THE THREE STEPS,

 Usually delineated upon the master's carpet, are emblematical of the three principal stages of human life, viz: *youth, manhood* and *age.* In *youth*, as entered apprentices, we ought industriously to occupy our minds in the attainment of useful knowledge: in *manhood*, as fellow crafts, we should apply our knowledge to the discharge of our respective duties to God, our neighbor, and ourselves; that so, in *age*, as master masons, we may enjoy the happy reflection consequent on a well-spent life, and die in the hope of a glorious immortality.

THE POT OF INCENSE

Is an emblem of a pure heart, which is always an acceptable sacrifice to the Deity ; and, as this glows with fervent heat, so should our hearts continually glow with gratitude to the great and beneficent Author of our existence, for the manifold blessings and comforts we enjoy

THE BEE HIVE

Is an emblem of industry, and recommends the practice of that virtue to all created beings, from the highest seraph in heaven, to the lowest reptile of the dust.— It teaches us, that as we came into the world rational and intelligent beings, so we should ever be industrious ones; never sitting down contented while our fellow-creatures around us are in want, especially when it is in our power to relieve them, without inconvenience to ourselves.

When we take a survey of nature, we view man, in his infancy, more helpless and indigent than the brutal creation ; he lies languishing for days, months and years, totally incapable of providing sustenance for himself, of guarding against the attack of the wild beasts of the field, or sheltering himself from the inclemencies of the weather. It might have pleased the great Creator of heaven

and earth, to have made man independent of all
other beings; but, as dependence is one of the
strongest bonds of society, mankind were made
dependent on each other for protection and security,
as they thereby enjoy better opportunities of ful
filling the duties of reciprocal love and friendship,
Thus was man formed for social and active life.
the noblest part of the work of God; and he that
will so demean himself, as not to be endeavoring to
add to the common stock of knowledge and understanding, may be deemed a *drone* in the *hive* of
nature, a useless member of society, and unworthy
of our protection as masons.

THE BOOK OF CONSTITUTIONS, GUARDED BY THE TYLER'S SWORD,

Reminds us that we should be ever
watchful and guarded in our thoughts
words and actions, particularly when
before the enemies of masonry; ever
bearing in remembrance those truly
masonic virtues, *silence* and *circumspection*.

THE SWORD, POINTING TO A NAKED HEART,

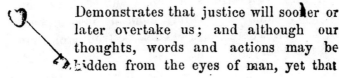

Demonstrates that justice will sooner or
later overtake us; and although our
thoughts, words and actions may be
hidden from the eyes of man, yet that

All-seeing Eye

whom the SUN, MOON, and STARS obey, and under
whose watchful care, even COMETS perform their
stupendous revolutions, pervades the inmost recesses
of the human HEART, and will reward us according
to our merits

THE ANCHOR AND ARK

Are emblems of a
well-grounded *hope*,
and a well-spent life.
They are emblem-
atical of that divine
Ark, which safely wafts us
over this tempestuous sea of troubles, and that
Anchor, which shall safely moor us into a peaceful harbor, where the wicked cease from troubling,
and the weary shall find rest.

THE FORTY-SEVENTH PROBLEM OF EUCLID.

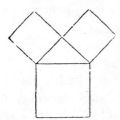

This was an invention of our ancient friend and brother, the great Pythagoras, who, in his travels through Asia, Africa and Europe, was initiated into several orders of priesthood, and raised to the sublime degree of a master mason. This wise philosopher enriched his mind abundantly in a general knowledge of things, and more especially in geometry, or masonry. On this subject, he drew out many problems and theorems; and among the most distinguished, he erected this, which, in the joy of his heart, he called *Eureka*, signifying, in the Grecian language, *I have found it;* and upon the discovery of which, he is said to have sacrificed a hecatomb. It teaches masons to be general lovers of the arts and sciences.

THE HOUR-GLASS

Is an emblem of human life. Behold! how swiftly the sands run, and how rapidly our lives are drawing to a close! We cannot without astonishment behold the little particles which are contained in this machine;—how they pass away almost imperceptibly! and yet, to our surprise, in the short space of an hour they are all exhausted. Thus wastes man! To-day, he puts forth the tender leaves of hope; to-morrow, blossoms and bears his blushing honors thick upon him; the next day comes a frost, which nips the shoot; and when he thinks his greatness is still aspiring, he falls, like autumn leaves, to enrich our mother earth.

THE SCYTHE

Is an emblem of time, which cuts the brittle thread of life, and launches us into eternity. Behold! what havoc the scythe of time makes among the human race! If by chance we should escape the numerous evils incident to childhood and youth, and with health and vigor arrive to the years of manhood; yet, withal, we must soon be cut down by the all-devouring scythe of time, and be gathered into the land where our fathers have gone before us.

*   *   *   *   *   *   *   *

Thus we close the explanation of the emblems upon the solemn thought of death, which, without revelation, is dark and gloomy; but the Christian is suddenly revived by the *ever-green* and ever living *sprig* of Faith in the merits of the Lion of the tribe of Judah; which strengthens him, with confidence and composure, to look forward to a blessed immortality; and doubts not, but in the glorious morn of the resurrection, his body will rise, and become as incorruptible as his soul.

Then let us imitate the Christian in his virtuous and amiable conduct; in his unfeigned piety to God; in his inflexible fidelity to his trust; that w may welcome the grim tyrant Death, and receive him as a kind messenger sent from our Supreme Grand Master, to translate us from this imperfect to that all-perfect, glorious and celestial Lodge above, where the Supreme Architect of the universe presides.

CHARGE TO THE CANDIDATE.

BROTHER:—Your zeal for our institution, the progress you have made in our mysteries, and your steady conformity to our useful regulations, have pointed you out as a proper object for this peculiar mark of our favor.

Duty and honor now alike bind you to be faithful to every trust; to support the dignity of your character on all occasions; and strenuously to enforce, by precept and example, a steady obedience to the tenets of Free-masonry. Exemplary conduct on your part, will convince the world, that merit is the just title to our privileges, and that on you our favors have not been undeservedly bestowed

In this respectable character you are authorized
to correct the irregularities of your less informed
brethren ; to fortify their minds with resolution
against the snares of the insidious, and to guard
them against every allurement to vicious practices.
To preserve unsullied the reputation of the fraternity, ought to be your constant care ; and, therefore, it becomes your province to caution the
inexperienced against a breach of fidelity. To
your inferiors in rank or office, you are to recommend obedience and submission ; to your equals,
courtesy and affability ; to your superiors, kindness
and condescension. Universal benevolence you are
zealously to inculcate ; and by the regularity of
your own conduct, endeavor to remove every
aspersion against this venerable institution. Our
ancient landmarks you are carefully to preserve,
and not suffer them, on any pretence, to be in-
fringed, or countenance a deviation from our
established customs.

Your honor and reputation are concerned in
supporting with dignity, the respectable character
you now bear. Let no motive, therefore, make you
swerve from your duty, violate your vows, or betray
your trust ; but be true and faithful, and imitate
the example of that celebrated artist whom you
have this evening represented. Thus you will
render yourself deserving of the honor which we
nave conferred, and worthy of the confidence we
nave reposed in you.

THE CHAPTER DEGREES.

MARK MASTER.

HIS degree of Masonry was not less useful in its original institution, nor are its effects less beneficial to mankind, than those which precede it   By the influence of this degree, each operative Mason, at the erection of the Temple of Solomon, was known and distinguished by the Senior Warden.   By its effects the disorder and confusion, that might otherwise have attended

so immense an undertaking was completely pre-
vented; and not only the craftsmen themselves, who
were eighty thousand in number, but every part
of their workmanship, was discriminated with the
greatest nicety, and the utmost facility. If defects
were found in the work, by the help of this degree,
the Overseers were enabled, without difficulty, to
ascertain who was the faulty workman; so that its
deficiencies might be remedied without injuring the
credit, or diminishing the reward of the industrious
and faithful of the craft.

CHARGE AT OPENING.

"Wherefore, brethren, lay
aside all malice, and guile,
and hypocrisies, and envies,
and all evil speakings. If
so be ye have tasted that
the Lord is gracious; to
whom coming, as unto a
living stone, disallowed in-
deed of men, but chosen of GOD, and precious; ye
also, as living stones, be ye built up a spiritual
house, an holy priesthood, to offer up sacrifices ac
ceptable to GOD.

"Brethren, this is the will of GOD, that, with well-
doing, ye put to silence the ignorance of foolish men
As free, and not as using your liberty for a cloak of
maliciousness; but as the servants of GOD.   Honor
all men; love the brotherhood; fear GOD."

SECTION I.

This section explains the manner of opening the lodge. It also teaches the stations* and duties of the officers, and the preparation and introduction of andidates.

---

* A Mark Master's Lodge, when fully organized for work, consists the members of the Chapter to which it is attached, and the following off cers, viz: R. W. Master, in the East; W. Senior Warden, in the West W. Junior Warden, in the South; Treasurer, on the right, and Secre tary, on the left, near the chair; Marshal, or Master of Ceremonies, o

In this section is exemplified the regularity and good order that was observed by the craftsmen on Mount Libanus, and in the plains and quarries of Zeredatha, and ends with a beautiful display of the manner in which one of the principal events originated, which characterizes this degree.

SECTION II.

Illustrates the foundation and history of the degree, and impresses upon the mind of the candidate, in a striking manner, the importance of a strict observance of his obligation to be ever ready to stretch forth his hand for the relief of indigent and worthy brethren. The number of workmen employed in building the Temple of Solomon, and the privileges they enjoyed, are specified; the mode of rewarding

the left, in front of the Secretary; Senior Deacon, on the right, in front of the Treasurer; Junior Deacon, at the right of the Senior Warden; Master Overseer, at the East Gate; Senior Overseer, at the West Gate; Junior Overseer, at the South Gate; Stewards, on the right and left of the Junior Warden; Chaplain, in the East, on the left of the Master.

The officers of Chapters take rank in Mark Master's Lodges as follows, viz: the High Priest, as R. W. Master; King, as Senior Warden; Scribe, as Junior Warden; Captain of the Host, as Marshal, or Master of Ceremonies; Principal Sojourner, as Senior Deacon; Royal Arch Captain, as Junior Deacon; Master of the Third Veil, as Master Overseer; Master of the Second Veil, as Senior Overseer; Master of the First Veil, as Junior Overseer. The Treasurer, Secretary, Chaplain, Stewards, and Tyler, as officers of corresponding rank.

merit, and of punishing the guilty, are pointed out; and the marks of distinction, which were conferred on our ancient brethren, as the rewards of excellence, are named.

* * * * * * * *

The following passages of Scripture are introduced and explained.

The stone which the builders refused, is become the head stone of the corner.—PSALMS cxviii. 22.

Did ye never read in the scriptures, The stone which the builders rejected, the same is become the head of the corner?—MATT. xxi. 42.

And have ye not read this scripture, The stone which the builders rejected, is become the head of the corner?—MARK xii. 10.

What is this then that is written, The stone which the builders rejected, the same is become the head of the corner?—LUKE xx. 17.

This is the stone which was set at naught of you builders, which is become the head of the corner.—ACTS iv. 11.

He that hath an ear to hear, let him hear.—REV. iii. 13.

To him that overcometh will I give to eat of the hidden manna, and I will give him a white stone, and in the stone a new name written, which no man knoweth saving he that receiveth it.—REV. ii. 17

And we will cut wood out of Lebanon, as much as thou shalt need; and we will bring it to thee in floats by sea to Joppa, and thou shalt carry it up to Jerusalem.—II CHRON. ii. 16.

Then he brought me back the way of the gate of the outward sanctuary, which looketh toward the east; and it was shut. And the Lord said unto me, Son of man, MARK WELL, and behold with thine eyes, and hear with thine ears all that I say unto thee concerning all the ordinances of the house of the Lord, and all the laws thereof; and mark well the entering in of the house, with every going forth of the sanctuary.—EZEKIEL xliv. 1–5.

* * * * * * * *

The *working tools* of a Mark Master are the *chisel* and *mallet*.

THE CHISEL

Morally demonstrates the advantages of discipline and education. The mind, like the diamond in its original state, is rude and unpolished; but as the effect of the chisel on the external coat soon presents to view the latent beauties of the diamond, so education discovers the latent virtues of the mind, and draws them forth to range the large field of matter and space, to display the summit of human knowledge, our duty to God and to man.

THE MALLET

Morally teaches to correct irregularities, and reduce man to a proper level; so that, by quiet deportment, he may, in the school of discipline, learn to be content. What the mallet is to the workman enlightened reason is to the passions: it curbs ambition; it depresses envy; it moderates anger, and it encourages good dispositions; whence arises among good masons that comely order,

" Which nothing earthly gives, or can destroy,
    The soul's calm sunshine, and the heartfelt joy "

THE FOLLOWING SONG MAY BE SUNG.

Music—" *God save great Washington.*"

Mark Masters all appear,
Before the Chief O'erseer,
        In concert move;

Let him your work inspect,
For the Chief Architect;
If there be no defect,
    He will approve

You who have passed the square,
For your rewards prepare,
    Join heart and hand;
Each with his mark in view,
March with the just and true;
Wages to you are due,
    At your command.

HIRAM, the widow's son,
Sent unto Solomon
    Our great key-stone;

On it appears the name
Which raises high the fame
Of all to whom the same
    Is truly known.

Now to the westward move,
Where, full of strength and love,
    HIRAM doth stand;
But if impostors are
Mix'd with the worthy there,
Caution them to beware
    Of the right hand.

*   *   *   *   *   *   *

THE FOLLOWING PARABLE IS RECITED.

For the kingdom of heaven is like unto a man that is an householder, which went out early in the morning to hire laborers into his vineyard. And when he had agreed with the laborers for a penny a day, he sent them into his vineyard. And he went out about the third hour, and saw others standing idle in the market-place, and said unto them, Go ye also into the vineyard; and whatsoever is right I will give you. And they went their way. And again he went out about the sixth and ninth hour, and did likewise. And about the eleventh hour, he went out and found others standing idle, and saith unto them, Why stand ye here all the day idle? They say unto him, Because no man hath hired us. He saith unto them, Go ye also into the

vineyard; and whatsoever is right, that shall ye receive. So when even was come, the lord of the vineyard saith unto his steward, Call the laborers, and give them their hire, beginning from the last unto the first. And when they came that were hired about the eleventh hour, they received every man a penny. But when the first came, they supposed that they should have received more; and they likewise received every man a penny. And when they had received it, they murmured against the good man of the house, saying, These last have wrought but one hour, and thou hast made them equal unto us, which have borne the burden and heat of the day. But he answered one of them, and said,

Friend, I do thee no wrong; didst not thou agree
with me for a penny? Take that thine is, and go thy
way; I will give unto this last, even as unto thee.
Is it not lawful for me to do what I will with mine
own? Is thine eye evil because I am good? So
the last shall be first, and the first last: for many
be called, but few chosen.—MATT. xx. 1–16.

* * * * * * * *

Now to the praise of those
Who triumph'd o'er the foes
Of mason's art;
To the praiseworthy three,
Who founded this degree;
May all their virtues be
Deep in our hearts.

CHARGE TO THE CANDIDATE.

BROTHER :—I congratulate you on having been
thought worthy of being promoted to this honorable
degree of Masonry. Permit me to impress it on
your mind, that your assiduity should ever be com-
mensurate with your duties, which become more
and more extensive as you advance in Masonry.

The situation to which you are now promoted,
will draw upon you not only the scrutinizing eyes
of the world at large, but those also of your breth-
en, on whom this degree of Masonry has not been

conferred ; all will be justified in expecting your conduct and behavior to be such as may with safety be imitated.

In the honorable character of Mark Master Mason, it is more particularly your duty to endeavor to let your conduct in the lodge, and among your brethren, be such as may stand the test of the Grand Overseer's square, that you may not, like the unfinished and imperfect work of the negligent and unfaithful of former times, be rejected and thrown aside, as unfit for that spiritual building, that house not made with hands, eternal in the heavens.

While such is your conduct, should misfortunes assail you, should friends forsake you, should envy traduce your good name, and malice persecute you; yet may you have confidence, that among Mark Master Masons you will have friends who will administer relief to your distresses, and comfort in your afflictions ; ever bearing in mind, as a consolation under all the frowns of fortune, and as an encouragement to hope for better prospects, that *the stone which the builders rejected,* (possessing merits to them unknown) *became the chief stone of the corner.*

The ceremony of closing a lodge in this degree is peculiarly interesting. It teaches us the duty we owe to our brethren in particular, and the whole family of mankind in general, by ascribing praise to the meritorious, and dispensing rewards to the diligent and industrious

PRESENT OR PAST MASTER.

.H I S degree should be carefully studied, and well understood, by every Master of a Lodge It treats of the government of our society; the disposition of our rulers; and illustrates their requisite qualifications. It includes the ceremony of opening and closing lodges in the several preceding degrees; and also the forms of Installation and Consecration, in the Grand Lodge.

as well as private lodges. It comprehends the ceremonies at laying the foundation stones of public buildings, and also at dedications and at funerals, by a variety of particulars explanatory of those ceremonies.

SECTION I

ON THE MANNER OF CONSTITUTING A LODGE.

Any number of Master Masons, not under seven, desirous of forming a new Lodge, must apply, by petition, to the Grand Lodge of the State in which they reside, as follows:

FORM OF A PETITION FOR A NEW LODGE.

"*To the M W. Grand Lodge of the State of* ——.

The undersigned petitioners, being Ancient Free and Accepted Master Masons, having the prosperity of the fraternity at heart, and willing to exert their best endeavors to promote and diffuse the genuine principles of Masonry, respectfully represent—That they are desirous of forming a new lodge in the —— of ——, to be named ——, No.—. They therefore pray for letters of dispensation, or a warrant of constitution, to empower them to assemble as a legal Lodge, to discharge the duties of Masonry, in a regular and constitutional manner, according to the original forms of the Order, and the regulations of the Grand Lodge. They have nominated and do recommend brother A. B to be the first Master; C. D to be the first Senior Warden, and E. F. to be the first Junior Warden, of said Lodge. If the prayer of the petition shall be granted, they promise a strict conformity to the constitution, laws and regulations of the Grand Lodge." *

---

* This petition, being signed by at least seven regular masons, and recommended by a lodge or lodges adjacent to the place where the new lodge is to be holden, is delivered to the Grand Secretary, who lays it before the Grand Lodge.

If the petition meets the approbation of the Grand Lodge, they generally order a dispensation to be issued, which is signed by the Grand or Deputy Grand Master, and authorizes the petitioners to assemble as a LEGAL lodge, for a specified term of time.

In some jurisdictions, the Grand and Deputy Grand Masters, respectively, are invested with authority to grant dispensations, at pleasure, during the recess of the Grand Lodge; in others, they are never issued without the special direction of the Grand Lodge.

Lodges working under dispensations are considered merely as agents of the Grand Lodge; their presiding officers are not entitled to the rank of Past Masters; their officers are not privileged with a vote or voice in the Grand Lodge; they cannot change their officers without the special approbation and appointment of the Grand Lodge; and in case of the cessation of such lodges, their funds, jewels, and other property accumulated by initiations into the several degrees, become the property of the Grand Lodge, and must be delivered over to the Grand Treasurer.

When lodges that are at first instituted by dispensation, have passed a proper term of probation, they make application to the Grand Lodge for a Charter of Constitution. If this be obtained, they are then confirmed in the possession of their property, and possess all the rights and privileges of regularly constituted lodges, as long as they conform to the Constitutions of Masonry. After a charter is granted by the Grand Lodge, the Grand Master appoints a day and hour for constituting and consecrating the new lodge, and for installing its master, wardens and other officers. If the Grand Master, in person, attends the ceremony, the lodge is said to be constituted in AMPLE FORM; if the Deputy Grand Master only, it is said to be constituted in DUE FORM; but if the power of performing the ceremony is vested in a subordinate lodge, it is said to be constituted in FORM.

When charters of constitution are granted for places where the distance is so great as to render it inconvenient for the grand officers to attend, the Grand Master, or his Deputy, issues a written instrument, under his hand and private seal, to some worthy Present or Past Master with full power to conjugate constitute and install the petitioners

CEREMONY OF CONSTITUTION

On the day and hour appointed, the Grand Master and his officers meet in a convenient room, near to that in which the lodge to be constituted is assembled, and open the Grand Lodge in the third degree of masonry.

The officers of the new lodge are to be examined by the Deputy Grand Master; after which they return to their lodge.

The new lodge then sends one of its members to the Grand Master, with the following message, viz:

"MOST WORSHIPFUL :—The officers and brethren of ——— Lodge, who are now assembled at ———, have instructed me to inform you, that the Most Worshipful Grand Lodge (or Grand Master) was pleased to grant them a letter of dispensation, bearing date the ——— day of ——— in the year ———, authorizing them to form and open a lodge of Free and Accepted Masons, in the ——— of ——— ; that since that period they have regularly assembled, and conducted the business of masonry according to the best of their abilities; that their proceedings, having received the approbation of the Most Worshipful Grand Lodge, they have obtained a Charter of Constitution, and are desirous that their lodge should be consecrated, and their officers installed, agreeably to the ancient usages and customs of the Craft; for which purpose they are now met, and await the pleasure of the Most Worshipful Grand Master "

He then returns to his lodge, who prepare for the reception of the Grand Lodge. When notice is given that they are prepared, the Grand Lodge walk in procession to their hall. When the Grand Master enters, the grand honors are given by the new lodge; the officers of which resign their seats to the grand officers, and take their several stations on their left.

The necessary cautions are then given, and all, excepting Masters and Past Masters of lodges, are requested to retire, until the Master of the new lodge is placed in the Oriental Chair. He is then bound to the faithful performance of his trust, and duly invested.

Upon due notice, the Grand Marshal reconducts the brethren into the hall, and all take their places, except the members of the new lodge, who form a procession on one side of the hall, to salute their Master. As they advance, the Grand Master addresses them, " *Brethren, Behold your Master!* " As they pass, they make the proper salutation, and when they have all passed, he joins them, and takes his appropriate station.

A grand procession is then formed in the following order, viz:

Tyler, with a drawn Sword:
Two Stewards, with White Rods;
Entered Apprentices;
Fellow Crafts;
Master Masons;

Stewards;
Junior Deacons;
Senior Deacons;
Secretaries;
Treasurers;
Past Wardens;
Junior Wardens;
Senior Wardens;
Past Masters;
Mark Masters;
Royal Arch Masons;
Knights Templars;
Masters of Lodges;

MARSHALS

THE NEW LODGE.

Tyler, with a drawn Sword;
Stewards, with White Rods;
Entered Apprentices;
Fellow Crafts;
Master Masons;
Deacons;
Secretary and Treasurer;
Two Brethren, carrying the Master's Carpet;
Junior and Senior Wardens;
The Holy Writings, carried by the oldest member
not in office;
The W. Master;
Music.

THE GRAND LODGE.

Grand Tyler, with a drawn Sword;

Grand Stewards, with White Rods ;
Brother, carrying a Golden Vessel with Corn ,
Two Brethren, carrying Silver Vessels, one of
Wine, the other of Oil ;
Grand Secretaries ;
Grand Treasurers ;
A Past Master, bearing the Holy Writings,
Square and Compasses, supported by two Stewarls,
with Rods ;
Two Burning Tapers, borne by two Past Masters ;
Clergy and Orator ;
The Tuscan and Composite Orders ;
The Doric, Ionic and Corinthian Orders ;
Past Grand Wardens ;
Past Deputy Grand Masters ;
Past Grand Masters ;
The Globes ;
Junior and Senior Grand Wardens ;
Right Worshipful Deputy Grand Master ;
The Master of the Oldest Lodge, carrying the
Book of Constitutions ;
The M. W. GRAND MASTER ;
The Grand Deacons, on a line seven feet apart, on
the right and left of the Grand Master, with
Black Rods ;
Grand Standard Bearer ;
Grand Sword Bearer, with a drawn Sword ;
Two Stewards, with White Rods.
The procession moves on to the church or house
where the services are to be performed.   When the

front of the procession arrives at the door, they halt, open to the right and left, and face inward, while the Grand Master, and others, in succession, pass through and ent█ the house.

A platform is erected in front of the pulpit, and provided with seats for the accommodation of the grand officers.

The Bible, Square and Compass, and Book of Constitutions, are placed upon a table in front of the Grand Master; the *Lodge* is placed in the centre, upon a platform, covered with white satin, or linen, and encompassed by the three tapers, and the vessels of corn, wine and oil.

SERVICES.

1 A piece of Music
2. Prayer.
3. An Oration.
4. A piece of Music.
5. The Grand Marshal then directs the officers and members of the new lodge in front of the Grand Master. The Deputy Grand Master addresses the Grand Master as follows:

"Most Worshipful:—A number of brethren, duly instructed in the mysteries of Masonry, having assembled together at stated periods, for some time past, by virtue of a dispensation granted them for that purpose, do now desire to be *constituted* into a *regular Lodge*, agreeably to the ancient usages and customs of the fraternity."

Their Secretary then delivers the dispensation and records to the Master elect, who presents them to the Grand Master.

The Grand Master examines the records, and if they are found correct, proclaims,

"The records appear to be properly entered, and are approved. Upon due deliberation, the Grand Lodge have granted the brethren of this new lodge, a Charter, confirming them in the rights and privileges of a *regularly constituted Lodge;* which the Grand Secretary will now read."

After the Charter is read, the Grand Master then says,

"We shall now proceed, according to ancient usage, to constitute these brethren into a regular lodge."

Whereupon the several officers of the new lodge deliver up their jewels and badges to their Master, who presents them with his own, to the Deputy Grand Master, and he to the Grand Master.

The Deputy Grand Master now presents the Master elect of the new lodge, to the Grand Master, saying,

"MOST WORSHIPFUL :—I present you Brother ——, whom the members of the lodge now to be constituted, have chosen for their Master."

The Grand Master asks them if they remain satisfied with their choice. (*They bow in token of assent.*)

The Master then presents, severally, his Wardens and other officers, naming them and their respective offices. The Grand Master asks the brethren if they remain satisfied with each and all of them. (*They bow as before.*)

The officers and members of the new lodge then form in the broad aisle, in front of the Grand Master, and the business of CONSECRATION commences with solemn music.

CEREMONY OF CONSECRATION.

The Grand Master, attended by the grand officers and the Grand Chaplain, form themselves in order, round the lodge, which is then uncovered, while a piece of solemn music is performed. The first clause of the Consecration Prayer is rehearsed, as follows:

"Great Architect of the Universe! Maker and Ruler of all Worlds! deign, from thy celestial temple, from realms of light and glory, to bless us in all the purposes of our present assembly!

"We humbly invoke thee to give us, at this and at all times, *Wisdom* in all our doings, *Strength* of mind in all our difficulties, and the *Beauty* of harmony in all our communications!

"Permit us, O thou Author of Light and Life, great Source of Love and Happiness, to erect this lodge, and now solemnly to *consecrate* it to the honor of thy glory!

" *Glory be to God on high*." Response.

" *As it was in the beginning, is now, and ever shall be! Amen*."

During the response, the Deputy Grand Master, and the Grand Wardens, take the vessels of corn, wine and oil, and sprinkle the elements of Consecration upon the Lodge.

The Grand Chaplain then continues :

" Grant, O Lord our God, that those who are now about to be invested with the government of this lodge, may be endued with wisdom to instruct their brethren in all their duties. May *Brotherly Love, Relief* and *Truth*, always prevail among the members of this lodge ; and may this bond of union continue to strengthen the lodges throughout the world !

" Bless all our brethren, wherever dispersed ; and grant speedy relief to all who are either oppressed or distressed.

" We affectionately commend to thee all the members of thy whole family. May they increase in the knowledge of thee, and in the love of each other.

" Finally; May we finish all our work here below, with thine approbation ; and then have our transition from this earthly abode to thy heavenly temple above, there to enjoy light, glory and bliss ineffable and eternal !

· *Glory be to God on high !*" Response.

A piece of solemn music is performed while the lodge is covered.

The Grand Chaplain then DEDICATES the Lodge in the following terms:

"To the memory of HOLY SAINTS JOHN we dedicate this Lodge. May every brother rever their character, and imitate their virtues.

   "*Glory be to God on high.*"
Response: "*Amen! so mote it be! Amen!*"

A piece of music is then performed, whilst the brethren of the new lodge advance in procession, to salute the Grand Lodge, with their hands crossed upon their breasts, and bowing as they pass.

The Grand Master then rises, and CONSTITUTES the new lodge in the form following:

"In the name of the Most Worshipful Grand Lodge, I now constitute and form you, my brethren, into a lodge of Free and Accepted Masons From henceforth I empower you to act as a regular lodge, constituted in conformity to the rites of our Order, and the charge of our ancient and honorable fraternity; and may the Supreme Architect of th universe prosper, direct and counsel you in all you doings."

Response: "*So mote it be!*"

SECTION II.

CEREMONY OF INSTALLATION.

The Grand Master* asks his Deputy, "Whether he has examined the Master nominated in the warrant, and finds him well skilled in the noble science and the royal art." The Deputy answering in the affirmative,† by the Grand Master's order, takes the candidate from among his fellows, and presents him at the pedestal, saying, "Most Worshipful Master, I present my worthy brother, A. B., to be installed Master of this (new) lodge. I find him to be of good morals, and of great skill, true and trusty; and I doubt not he will discharge his duty with fidelity."

The Grand Master then addresses him:

"BROTHER:—Previous to your investiture, it is necessary that you should signify your assent to those ancient charges and regulations which point out the duty of a Master of a Lodge."

The Grand Master then reads, or orders to be read, a summary of the ancient charges to the Master elect, as follows, viz:

I. You agree to be a good man and true, and strictly to obey the moral law.

---

* In this and other similar instances, where the Grand Master is specified in acting may be understood any Master who performs the ceremony.

† A private examination is understood to precede the installation of every officer.

II. You agree to be a peaceable citizen, and cheerfully to conform to the laws of the country in which you reside.

III. You promise not to be concerned in plots and conspiracies against government, but patiently to submit to the decisions of the supreme legislature.

IV. You agree to pay a proper respect to the civil magistrates, to work diligently, live creditably, and act honorably by all men.

V. You agree to hold in veneration the original rulers and patrons of the Order of Masonry, and their regular successors, supreme and subordinate, according to their stations; and to submit to the awards and resolutions of your brethren, when convened, in every case consistent with the constitutions of the Order.

VI. You agree to avoid private piques and quarrels, and to guard against intemperance and excess.

VII. You agree to be cautious in your behavior, courteous to your brethren, and faithful to your lodge.

VIII. You promise to respect genuine brethren and to discountenance imposters, and all dissenter from the original plan of Masonry.

IX. You agree to promote the general good of society; to cultivate the social virtues, and to propagate the knowledge of the art.

X. You promise to pay homage to the Grand Master for the time being, and to his officers when duly installed; and strictly to conform to every edict of the Grand Lodge, or General Assembly of Masons, that is not subversive of the principles and ground work of Masonry.

XI. You admit that it is not in the power of any man, or body of men, to make innovations in the body of Masonry.

XII. You promise a regular attendance on the committees and communications of the Grand Lodge, on receiving proper notice; and to pay attention to all the duties of Masonry, on convenient occasions.

XIII. You admit that no new lodge shall be formed without permission of the Grand Lodge; and that no countenance be given to any irregular lodge, or to any person clandestinely initiated therein, being contrary to the ancient charges of the Order.

XIV. You admit that no person can be regularly made a Mason in, or admitted a member of, any regular lodge, without previous notice, and due inquiry into his character.

XV. You agree that no visitors shall be received into your lodge without due examination, and producing proper vouchers of their having been initiated into a regular lodge.

These are the regulations of Free and Accepted Masons

The Grand Master then addresses the Master elect in the following manner: "Do you submit to

these charges, and promise to support these regulations, as Masters have done in all ages before
you ? "

The Master having signified his cordial submission as before, the Grand Master thus addresses
him :—

" Brother A. B., in consequence of your conformity to the charges and regulations of the Order,
you are now to be installed Master of this lodge,
in full confidence of your care, skill and capacity
to govern the same."

The Master is then regularly invested
with the insignia of his office, and the
furniture and implements of his lodge.
The various implements of the profession are
emblematical of our conduct in life, and upon this
occasion are carefully enumerated.

The *Holy Writings*, that great light in
Masonry, will guide you to all truth ; it
will direct your paths to the temple of happiness,
and point out to you the whole duty of man.

The *Square* teaches us to regulate
our actions by rule and line, and to
harmonize our conduct by the principles of morality and virtue.

The *Compass* teaches us to limit our desires in every station, that, rising to eminence
by merit, we may live respected, and die regretted.

The *Rule* directs, that we should punctually observe our duty ; press forward in the path of virtue, and, neither inclining to the right nor to the left, in all our actions have *eternity* in view.

The *Line* teaches us the criterion of moral rectitude, to avoid dissimulation in conversation and action, and to direct our steps to the path which leads to *immortality*.

The *Book of Constitutions* you are to search at all times. Cause it to be read in your lodge, that none may pretend ignorance of the excellent precepts it enjoins.

You now receive in charge the *Charter*, by the authority of which this lodge is held. You are carefully to preserve and duly transmit it to your successor in office.

Lastly, you receive in charge the *By-Laws* of your lodge, which you are to see carefully and punctually executed.

The Jewels of the officers of the new lodge are then returned to the Master, who delivers them, respectively, to the several officers of the Grand Lodge, according to their rank.

The subordinate officers of the new lodge are then invested with their jewels, by the grand officers of corresponding rank ; and are by them, severally in turn, conducted to the Grand Master, who delivers to each of them a short charge, as follows :—

THE SENIOR WARDEN.

" Brother C. D., you are appointed* Senior Warden of this lodge, and are now invested with the insignia of your office.

" The *Level* demonstrates that we are descended from the same stock, partake of the same nature, and share the same hope ; and though distinctions among men are necessary to preserve subordination, yet no eminence of station should make us forget that we are brethren ; for he who is placed on the lowest spoke of fortune's wheel, may be entitled to our regard ; because a time will come, and the wisest knows not how soon, when all distinctions, but that of goodness, shall cease ; and death, the grand leveler of human greatness, reduce us to the same state.

" Your regular attendance on our stated meetings is essentially necessary. In the absence of the Master, you are to govern this lodge ; in his presence, you are to assist him in the government of it. I firmly rely on your knowledge of Masonry, and attachment to the lodge for the faithful discharge of the duties of this important trust —*Look well to the West !*"

---

* When the Installation is not of the officers of a new lodge, the words " have been elected," should be substituted for the words " are appointed," in all cases where the officer is chosen by ballot.

THE JUNIOR WARDEN.

" Brother E. F., you are appointed Junior Warden of this lodge ; and are now invested with the badge of your office.

The *Plumb* admonishes us to walk uprightly in our several stations, to hold the scale of justice in equal poise ; to observe the just medium between intemperance and pleasure, and to make our passions and prejudices coincide with the line of our duty. To you is committed the superintendence of the craft during the hours of refreshment ; it is therefore indispensably necessary that you should not only be temperate and discreet in the indulgence of your own inclinations, but carefully observe that none of the craft be suffered to convert the purposes of refreshment into intemperance and excess. Your regular and punctual attendance is particularly requested, and I have no doubt that you will faithfully execute the duty which you owe to your present appointment. — *Look well to the South !* "

THE TREASURER

" Brother G. H., you are appointed Treasurer of this lodge. It is your duty to receive all moneys from the hands of the Secretary ; keep just and regular accounts of the same, and pay them out at the Worshipful Master's will and pleasure, with the consent of the lodge. I trust your regard for the fraternity will prompt you to the faithful discharge of the duties of your office "

THE SECRETARY.

"Brother I. K., you are appointed Secretary of this lodge. It is your duty to observe the Worshipful Master's will and pleasure; to record the proceedings of the lodge, to receive all moneys, and pay them into the hands of the Treasurer. Your good inclination to Masonry and this lodge, I hope, will induce you to discharge the duties of your office with fidelity, and by so doing, you will merit the esteem and applause of your brethren."

THE CHAPLAIN.

"Rev. Brother L. M., you are appointed Chaplain of this lodge. It is your duty to perform those solemn services which we should constantly render to our infinite Creator; and which, when offered by one whose holy profession is "to point to heaven and lead the way," may, by refining our souls, strengthening our virtues, and purifying our minds, prepare us for admission into the society of those above, whose happiness will be as endless as it is perfect."

THE SENIOR AND JUNIOR DEACONS.

"Brothers L. M. and N. O., you are appointed Deacons of this lodge. It is your province to attend on the Master and Wardens, and to act as their proxies in the active duties of the lodge; such as in the reception of candidates into the different degrees of Masonry; the introduction and accommodation of visitors, and in the immediate practice of our rites. The Square and Compasses, as badges of your office, I entrust to your care, not doubting your vigilance and attention."

THE STEWARDS, OR MASTERS OF CEREMONIES.*

"Brothers R. S. and T. U., you are appointed Stewards (Masters of Ceremonies) [STEWARDS.] of this lodge. The duties of [M's of C's.] your office are to assist the Deacons and other officers in performing their respective duties. Your regular and early attendance will afford the best proof of your zeal and attachment to the lodge."

THE TYLER.

"Brother V. W., you are appointed Tyler of this lodge, and I invest you with the implement of your office. As the sword is placed in the hands of the Tyler, to enable him effectually to guard against the approach of cowans and eavesdroppers, and suffer none to pass or repass but such as are duly qualified, so it should admonish us to set a guard over our thoughts, a watch at our lips, post a sentinel over our actions; thereby

---

* Many lodges have abolished the title of Stewards, and substituted that of Masters of Ceremonies, who perform the duties appertaining to the former

preventing the approach of every unworthy thought or deed, and preserving consciences void of offence towards GOD and towards man."

CHARGE UPON THE INSTALLATION OF THE OFFICERS OF A LODGE.

"WORSHIPFUL MASTER :—The Grand Lodge having committed to your care the superintendence and government of the brethren who are to compose this lodge, you cannot be insensible of the obligations which devolve on you as their head; nor of your responsibility for the faithful discharge of the important duties annexed to your appointment. The honor, reputation and usefulness of your lodge, will materially depend on the skill and assiduity with which you manage its concerns; whilst the happiness of its members will be generally promoted, in proportion to the zeal and ability with which you propagate the genuine principles of our institution.

" For a pattern of imitation, consider the great luminary of nature, which, rising in the *East*, regularly diffuses light and lustre to all within the circle. In like manner it is your province to spread and communicate light and instruction to the brethren of your lodge. Forcibly impress upon them the dignity and high importance of Masonry; and seriously admonish them never to disgrace it. Charge them to practice *out* of the lodge, those duties which they have been taught in it; and by amiable, discreet and virtuous conduct, to convince mankind of the goodness of the institution; so that when a person is said to be a member of it, the world may know that he is one to whom the burthened heart may pour out its sorrows; to whom distress may prefer its suit; whose hand is guided by justice, and his heart is expanded by benevolence. In short, by a diligent observance of the By-laws of your lodge, the Constitutions of Masonry, and above all, the Holy Scriptures, which are given as a rule and guide to your faith, you will be enabled to acquit yourself with honor and reputation, and lay up a *crown of rejoicing*, which shall continue when time shall be no more.

" BROTHER SENIOR AND JUNIOR WARDENS :

" You are too well acquainted with the principles of Masonry, to warrant any distrust that you will be found wanting in the discharge of your respective duties. Suffice it to say, that what you have seen praiseworthy in others, you should carefully imitate; and what in them may have appeared defective, you should in yourselves amend. You should be examples of good order and regularity; for it is only by a due regard to the laws, in your own conduct, that you can expect obedience to them from others. You are assiduously to assist the Master in the discharge of his trust; diffusing light and imparting knowledge to all whom he shall place under your care. In the absence of the

Master, you will succeed to higher duties; your acquirements must therefore be such, as that the craft may never suffer for want of proper instruction. From the spirit which you have hitherto evinced, I entertain no doubt that your future conduct will be such as to merit the applause of your brethren, and the testimony of a good conscience.

" Brethren of ——— Lodge :

" Such is the nature of our constitution, that as some must of necessity rule and teach, so others must, of course, learn to submit and obey. Humility in both is an essential duty. The officers who are appointed to govern your lodge, are sufficiently conversant with the rules of propriety, and the laws of the institution, to avoid exceeding the powers with which they are entrusted; and you are of too generous dispositions to envy their preferment. I therefore trust that you will have but one aim, to please each other, and unite in the grand design of being happy and communicating happiness.

"Finally, my brethren, as this association has been formed and perfected in so much unanimity and concord, in which we greatly rejoice, so may it long continue. May you long enjoy every satisfaction and delight, which disinterested friendship can afford. May kindness and brotherly affection distinguish your conduct, as men and as masons. Within your peaceful walls, may your childrens' children celebrate with joy and gratitude, the annual recurrence of this auspicious solemnity. And may the *tenets of our profession* be transmitted through your lodge, pure and unimpaired, from generation to generation."

The Grand Marshal then proclaims the new lodge, in the following manner, viz:

"In the name of the Most Worshipful Grand Lodge of the State of ———, I proclaim this new Lodge, by the name of ——— Lodge, duly constituted."

The Grand Chaplain then makes the concluding prayer, which ends the public ceremonies.

The grand procession is then formed in the same order as before, and returns to the hall. The following, or some other ode, is sung, which concludes the ceremony of installation.

INSTALLATION ODE.
Music—"Bright Rosy Morning."

Behold! in the East our new Master appear;
Come, brothers, we'll greet him with hearts all
    sincere;
We'll serve him with freedom, fervor and zeal;
And aid him his duties and trust to fulfil.

In the West see the Warden with Level in hand,
The Master to aid, and obey his command,
We'll aid him with freedom, fervor and zeal,
And help him his duties and trust to fulfil.

In the South, see the Warden by Plumb stand
    upright,
Who watches the sun, and takes note of its flight,
We'll aid, &c.

The lodge is then closed with the usual solemnities in the different degrees, by the Grand Master and his officers.

This is the usual ceremony observed by regular Masons at the Constitution of a new lodge, which the Grand Master may abridge or extend at pleasure; but the material points are upon no account to be omitted. The same ceremony and charges attend every succeeding installation of new officers.

SECTION III.

CEREMONY AT LAYING FOUNDATION STONES OF PUBLIC STRUCTURES

HIS ceremony is conducted by the Grand Master and his officers, assisted by the members of the Grand Lodge, and such officers and members of private lodges as can conveniently attend. The Chief Magistrate, and other civil officers of the place where the building is to be erected, also generally attend on the occasion.

At the time appointed, the Grand Lodge is convened in some suitable place, approved by the Grand Master. A band of martial music is pro vided, and the brethren appear in the insignia of the Order, and with white gloves and aprons. The lodge is opened by the Grand Master, and the rules for regulating the procession to and from the place where the ceremony is to be performed, are read by the Grand Secretary. The necessary cautions are then given from the Chair, and the lodge is adjourned; after which the procession sets out in the following order:

PROCESSION AT LAYING FOUNDATION STONES.

Two Tylers, with drawn Swords;
Tyler of the oldest Lodge, with a drawn Sword;
Two Stewards of the oldest Lodge;
Entered Apprentices;
Fellow Crafts;
Master Masons;
Stewards;
Junior Deacons;
Senior Deacons;
Secretaries;
Treasurers;
Past Wardens;
Junior Wardens;
Senior Wardens;
Past Masters;
Mark Masters;
Royal Arch Masons;
Knights Templars;
Masters of Lodges;

MARSHALS

Music ;
Grand Tyler, with a drawn Sword ;
Grand Stewards, with White Rods ;
A Brother, with a Golden Vessel containing Corn ;
Two Brethren, carrying Silver Vessels, one of
Wine, the other of Oil ;
Principal Architect, with Square, Level and Plumb;
Grand Secretary ;
Grand Treasurer ;
Bible, Square and Compass, carried by a Master
of a Lodge, supported by two Stewards ;
Grand Chaplain ;
The Five Orders ;
Past Grand Wardens ;
Past Deputy Grand Masters ;
Past Grand Masters ;
Chief Magistrate of the place ;
Two Large Lights, borne by two Masters of Lodges;
Grand Wardens ;
Deputy Grand Master ;
The Master of the Oldest Lodge, carrying the
Book of Constitutions ;
Grand Deacons, with Black Rods, seven feet apart·
The M. W. GRAND MASTER ;
Grand Standard Bearer ;
Grand Sword Bearer, with a drawn Sword ;
Two Stewards, with White Rods.

A triumphal arch is usually erected at the place
where the ceremony is to be performed. The procession passes through the arch, and the brethren

repairing to their stands, the Grand Master and his officers take their places on a temporary platform, covered with carpet.

An ode in honor of Masonry is then sung.

The Grand Master commands silence, and the necessary preparations are made for laying the stone, on which is engraved the year of Masonry, the name and titles of the Grand Master, &c., &c.

The stone is raised up, by the means of an engine erected for that purpose, and the Grand Chaplain, or Orator, repeats a short prayer. The Grand Treasurer, by the Grand Master's command, places under the stone various sorts of coin and medals of the present age. Solemn music is introduced, and the stone let down into its place. The principal Architect then presents the working tools to the Grand Master, who applies the *Plumb, Square and Level* to the stone, in their proper positions, and pronounces it to be " WELL FORMED, TRUE AND TRUSTY."

The golden and silver vessels are next brought to the table, and delivered; the former to the Deputy Grand Master, and the latter to the Grand Wardens, who successively present them to the Grand Master; and he, according to ancient ceremony, pours the corn, the wine, and the oil, which they contain, on the stone; saying.

"May the all-bounteous Author of Nature bless the inhabitants of this place with all the necessaries, conveniences and comforts of life; assist in

the erection and completion of this building ; pro
tect the workmen against every accident, and lon;
preserve this structure from decay ; and grant t
us all, a supply of the CORN of *nourishment*, th
WINE of *refreshment*, and the OIL of *joy*."

"*Amen! so mote it be! Amen!*"

He then strikes the stone thrice with the mallet,
and the public honors of masonry are given.

The Grand Master then delivers over to the Ar
chitect the various implements of architecture
entrusting him with the superintendence and direc
tion of the work ; after which he reascends the
platform, and an oration, suitable to the occasion
is delivered. A voluntary collection is made for
the workmen, and the sum collected is placed upor
the stone by the Grand Treasurer. The ceremony
concludes with an appropriate ode. After which
the procession returns to the place whence it set
out, and the lodge is closed in due form.

SECTION IV.

CEREMONY AT THE DEDICATION OF MASONIC HALLS.

On the day appointed for the celebration of the
ceremony of Dedication, the Grand Master and his
officers, accompanied by the members of the Grand
Lodge meet in a convenient room, near to the place
where the ceremony is be performed, and the Grand
Lodge is opened in ample form, in the third degree
of Masonry.

The Master of the Lodge to which the hall to be dedicated belongs, being present, rises and addresses the Grand Master as follows :

" MOST WORSHIPFUL :

" The brethren of ———— Lodge, being animated with a desire of promoting the honor and interest of the craft, have, at great pains and expense, erected a Masonic Hall, for their convenience and accommodation. They are now desirous that the same should be examined by the Most Worshipful Grand Lodge ; and if it should meet their approbation, that it should be solemnly dedicated to Masonic purposes, agreeably to ancient form."

The Grand Master then directs the Grand Secretary to read the Order of Procession, which is delivered over to the Grand Marshal ; and a general charge, respecting propriety of behavior, is given by the Deputy Grand Master ; or the necessary directions are given to the brethren from the Chair

A grand procession is then formed in the order laid down in the first section. The whole moves forward to the hall which is to be dedicated ; and upon the arrival of the front of the procession at the door, they halt, open to the right and left, and face inward, whilst the Grand Master, and others in succession, pass through and enter. The music continues while the procession marches three times around the hall.

The Lodge is placed in the centre. The Grand

Master having taken the chair, under a canopy. the grand officers take the places of the corresponding officers of the lodge, and the Masters and Wardens of other lodges, repair to the places previously prepared for their reception. The three lights (in a triangular form), and the gold and silver pitchers, with the corn, wine and oil, are placed on the Lodge, at the head of which stands the pedestal, or altar, with the Bible open, and the Square and Compass fixed thereon, with the Charter, Book of Constitutions and By-laws.

An anthem is sung, and an exordium on Masonry given ; after which, the Architect addresses the Grand Master as follows:

"Most Worshipful:

"Having been entrusted with the superintendence and management of the workmen employed in the construction of this edifice ; and having, according to the best of my ability, accomplished the task assigned me, I now return my thanks for the honor of this appointment, and beg leave to surrender up the implements which were committed to my care, when the foundation of this fabric was laid ; humbly hoping, that the exertions which have been made on this occasion, will be crowned with your approbation, and that of the Most Worshipful Grand Lodge."

To which the Grand Master replies as follows:

"Brother Architect :—The skill and fidelity

displayed in the execution of the trust reposed in you, at the commencement of this undertaking, have secured the entire approbation of the Grand Lodge ; and they sincerely pray, that this edifice may continue a lasting monument of the taste, spirit, and liberality of its founders."

An ode in honor of Masonry is sung.

The Deputy Grand Master then rises and says:

" MOST WORSHIPFUL :—The hall in which we are now assembled, and the plan upon which it has been constructed, having met with your approbation, it is the desire of the fraternity that it should be now dedicated, according to ancient form and usage "

Whereupon the Grand Master requests all to retire but such as are Master Masons. A procession is then formed in the following order, viz :

Grand Sword Bearer ;

Grand Standard Bearer ;

A Past Master, with a Light ;

A Past Master, with Bible, Square and Compass
on a Velvet Cushion ;

Two Past Masters, each with a Light ;

Grand Secretary and Treasurer, with Emblems ;

Grand Junior Warden, with Pitcher of Corn :

Grand Senior Warden, with Pitcher of Wine ;

Deputy Grand Master, with Pitcher of Oil ;

Grand Master ;

Two Stewards, with Rods.

All the other brethren keep their places, **and** assist in performing an ode, which continues during the procession, excepting only at the intervals of dedication.

Music—"Migdol."

Genius of Masonry! descend,
And with thee bring thy spotless train;
Constant at our sacred rites attend,
While we adore thy peaceful reign.

The Lodge being uncovered, and the first procession being made around it, the Grand Master having reached the East, the Grand Junior Warden presents the pitcher of corn to the Grand Master, who, striking thrice with his mallet, pours it out upon the Lodge, at the same time pronouncing,

"In the name of the great Jehovah, to whom be all honor and glory, I do solemnly dedicate this hall to Free-masonry."

The grand honors are given.

Bring with thee Virtue! brightest maid;
Bring Love, bring Truth, bring Friendship here
While social mirth shall lend her aid,
To soothe the wrinkled brow of care.

The second procession is then made around the Lodge, and the Grand Senior Warden presents the pitcher of wine to the Grand Master, who sprinkles it upon the Lodge, at the same time saying,

" In the name of the Holy SAINTS JOHN, I do solemnly dedicate this hall to VIRTUE."

The grand honors are twice repeated.

Bring CHARITY ! with goodness crowned,
Encircled in thy heavenly robe !
Diffuse thy blessings all around,
To every corner of the GLOBE !

The third procession is then made round the Lodge, and the Deputy Grand Master presents the pitcher of oil to the Grand Master, who, sprinkling it upon the Lodge, says,

" In the name of the whole FRATERNITY, I do solemnly dedicate this hall to UNIVERSAL BENEV- OLENCE."

The grand honors are thrice repeated.

A solemn invocation is made to the Throne of Grace, by the Grand Chaplain.

To Heaven's high Architect all praise,
    All praise, all gratitude be given,
Who deigned the human soul to raise,
    By mystic secrets sprung from Heaven.

After which the Lodge is covered, and the Grand Master retires to his chair. An oration is then delivered, and the ceremonies conclude with music. The Grand Lodge is again formed in procession, as at first, and returns to the room where it was opened, and is closed in ample form.

SECTION V.

THE CEREMONY OBSERVED AT FUNERALS.

THE ceremonies which are ob
served on the occasion of fune
rals are highly appropriate
they are performed as a melan
choly Masonic duty, and as a
token of respect and affection to
the memory of a departed brother. No mason can be interred
with the formalities of the Or-
der unless he has been advanced to the third degree
Fellow Crafts and Apprentices are not entitled to
funeral obsequies. All the brethren who walk in
procession, should observe, as much as possible, an
uniformity in their dress; black clothes, with white
gloves and aprons, are most suitable.

The brethren being assembled at the Lodge
room, (or some other convenient place) the presiding officer opens the lodge in the third degree; and
having stated the purpose of the meeting, a procession is then formed, which moves to the house of the
deceased, and from thence to the place of interment.

NOTE.—If a past or present Grand Master, Deputy Grand Master, or
Grand Warden, should join the procession of a private lodge, proper
attention is to be paid to them. They take place after the Master of
the lodge. Two Deacons, with black rods, are appointed by the Master
to attend a Grand Warden; and when the Grand Master or Deputy
Grand Master is present, the Book of Constitutions is borne before
him, a Sword Bearer follows him, and the Deacons, with black rods, on
his right and left.

ORDER OF PROCESSION AT A FUNERAL.

Tyler, with a drawn Sword ;
Stewards, with White Rods ;
Musicians, (if they are Masons,) otherwise
they follow the Tyler ;
Master Masons ;
Senior and Junior Deacons ;
Secretary and Treasurer ;
Senior and Junior Wardens ;
Mark Masters ;
Past Masters ;
Royal Arch Masons ;
Select Masters ;
Knights Templars ;
The Holy Writings, on a cushion, covered with
black cloth, carried by the oldest (or some
suitable) member of the Lodge ;
The Master ;
Clergy ;

MARSHAL.

The   Body,

with the insignia   placed thereon.

Pall Bearers.   Pall Bearers.

When the procession arrives at the place of interment, the members of the lodge form a circle round the grave; the officers take their position at the head of the grave and the mourners at the foot. The following exhortation is ther given:

FUNERAL SERVICE AT THE GRAVE.

BRETHREN :—

‧ The solemn notes that betoken the dissolution of this earthly tabernacle, have again alarmed our outer door, and another spirit has been summoned to the land where our fathers have gone before us. Again we are called to assemble among the habitations of the dead, to behold the "narrow house appointed for all living." Here, around us, in that peace which the world cannot give, sleep the unnumbered dead. The gentle breeze fans their verdant covering, they heed it not ; the sunshine and the storm pass over them, and they are not disturbed ; stones and lettered monuments symbolize the affection of surviving friends, yet no sound proceeds from them, save that silent but thrilling admonition, "seek ye the narrow path and the straight gate that lead unto eternal life."

We are again called upon to consider the uncertainty of human life ; the immutable certainty of death, and the vanity of all human pursuits. Decrepitude and decay are written upon every living thing. The cradle and the coffin stand in juxtaposition to each other; and it is a melancholy truth, that so soon as we begin to live that moment also we begin to die. It is passing strange, that notwithstanding the daily mementos of mortality that cross our path; notwithstanding the funeral bell so often tolls in our ears, and the "mournful procession" go about our streets, that we will not more seriously consider our approaching fate. We go on from design to design, add hope to hope, and lay out plans for the employment of many years, until we are suddenly alarmed at the approach of the Messenger of Death, at a moment when we least expect him, and which we probably conclude to be the meridian of our existence.

What, then, are all the externals of human dignity, the power of wealth, the dreams of ambition, the pride of intellect, or the charms of beauty, when Nature has paid her just debt? Fix your eyes on the last sad scene, and view life stript of its ornaments, and exposed in its natural meanness, and you must be persuaded of the utter emptiness of these delusions In the grave all fallacies are detected, all ranks are leveled, and all distinctions are done away.

While we drop the sympathetic tear over the grave of our deceased brother, let us cast around his foibles, whatever they may have been, the *broad mantle of masonic charity,* nor withhold from his memory the commendation that his virtues claim at our hands. Perfection on earth has never yet been attained ; the wisest, as well as the best of men, have gone astray. Suffer, then, the apol ogies of human nature to plead for him who can no longer extenuate for himself.

Our present meeting and proceedings will have been vain and useless, if they fail to excite our serious reflections, and strengthen our resolutions of amendment. Be then persuaded, my brethren, by the uncertainty of human life, and the unsubstantial nature of all its pursuits, and no longer postpone the all-important concern of preparing for eternity. Let us each embrace the present moment, and while time and opportunity offer, prepare for that great change, when the pleasures of the world shall be as poison to our lips, and happy reflections of a well spent life afford the only consolation. Thus shall our hopes be not frustrated, nor we hurried unprepared into the presence of that all-wise and powerful Judge, to whom the secrets of every heart are known. Let us resolve to maintain with greater assiduity the dignified character of our profession. May our *faith* be evinced in a correct moral walk and deportment ; may our *hope* be bright as the glorious mysteries that will be revealed hereafter ; and our *charity* boundless as the wants of our fellow creatures. And having faithfully discharged the great luties which we owe to God, to our neighbor and ourselves; when at last it shall please the Grand Master of the universe to summon us into his eternal presence, may the *trestle-board* of our whole lives pass such inspection that it may be given unto each of us to " eat of the hidden manna," and to receive the " white stone with a new name written," that will ensure perpetual and unspeakable happiness at his right hand.

The Master then presenting the apron continues.

" The lamb-skin or white apron, is the emblem of innocence, and the badge of a Mason. It is more ancient than the golden fleece or Roman eagle ; more honorable than the star and garter, when worthily worn."

The Master then deposits it in the grave.

This emblem I now deposit in the grave of our deceased brother. By it we are reminded of the universal dominion of Death. The arm of Friendship cannot interpose to prevent his coming ; the wealth of the world cannot purchase our release ; nor will the innocence of youth, or the charms of beauty propitiate his purpose. The mattock, the coffin, and the melancholy grave, admonish us of our mortality, and that, sooner or later, these frail bodies must moulder in their parent dust.

The Master, holding the evergreen, continues.

This *evergreen*, which once marked the temporary resting place of the illustrious dead, is an emblem of our faith in the immortality of the soul.

By this we are reminded that we have an immortal part within us, that shall survive the grave, and which shall never, never, never die. By it we are admonished, that, though like our brother, whose remains lie before us, we shall soon be clothed in the habiliments of DEATH and deposited in the silent tomb, yet, through the merits of a divine and ascended SAVIOR, we may confidently hope that · our souls will bloom in eternal spring.

The brethren then move in procession round the place of interment, and severally drop the sprig of evergreen into the grave ; after which, the public grand honors are given. The Master then continues the ceremony at the grave, in the following words :

From time immemorial, it has been the custom among the fraternity of free and accepted Masons, at the request of a brother, to accompany his corpse to the place of interment, and there to deposit his remains with the usual formalities.

In conformity to this usage, and at the request of our deceased brother, whose memory we revere, and whose loss we now deplore, we have assembled in the character of masons, to offer up to his memory, before the world, the last tribute of our affection ; thereby demonstrating the sincerity of our past esteem for him, and our steady attachment to the principles of the order.

The Great Creator having been pleased, out of his infinite mercy, to remove our brother from the cares and troubles of this transitory existence, to a state of endless duration, thus severing another link from the fraternal chain that binds us together;

may we, who survive him, be more strongly ce-
mented in the ties of union and friendship; that,
during the short space allotted us here, we may
wisely and usefully employ our time; and, in the
reciprocal intercourse of kind and friendly acts,
mutually promote the welfare and happiness of each
other. Unto the grave we have consigned the body
of our deceased brother; earth to earth, ashes to
ashes, dust to dust; there to remain till the trump
shall sound on the resurrection morn. We can
cheerfully leave him in the hands of a Being, who
has done all things well; who is glorious in holiness, fearful in praises, doing wonders.

To those of his immediate relatives and friends,
who are most heart stricken at the loss we have all
sustained, we have but little of this world's consolation to offer. We can only sincerely, deeply and
most affectionately sympathize with them in their
afflictive bereavement. But in the beautiful spirit
of the Christian's theology we dare to say, that HE,
who "tempers the wind to the shorn lamb," looks
down with infinite compassion upon the widow and
fatherless, in the hour of their desolation; and that
the same benevolent Savior, who wept while on
earth, will fold the arms of his love and protection
around those who put their trust in HIM.

Then let us improve this solemn warning that at
last, when the "sheeted dead" are stirring, when
the "great white throne" is set, we shall receive
from the Omniscient Judge, the thrilling invitation,

Come, ye blessed of my Father, inherit the kingdom prepared for you from the foundation of the world.

The service is here concluded with the following, or some suitable prayer :

ALMIGHTY and most merciful Father, we adore thee as the God of time and of eternity. As it has pleased thee to take from the light of our abode, one dear to our hearts, we beseech thee to bless and sanctify unto us this dispensation of thy Providence. Inspire our hearts with wisdom from on high, that we may glorify thee in all our ways. May we realize that thine All-seeing Eye is upon us, and be influenced by the spirit of truth and love to perfect obedience,—that we may enjoy the divine approbation here below. And when our toils on earth shall have ceased, may we be raised to the enjoyment of fadeless light and immortal life in that kingdom where faith and hope shall end—and love and joy prevail through eternal ages.

And thine, O righteous Father, shall be the glory forever. Amen.

Thus the service ends, and the procession returns in form to the place whence it set out, where the necessary duties are complied with, and the business of Masonry is renewed. The insignia and ornaments of the deceased, if an officer of a lodge, are returned to the Master, with the usual ceremonies

MOST EXCELLENT MASTER.

ONE but the meritorious and praiseworthy; none but those who, through diligence and industry, have progressed far towards perfection; none but those who have been seated in the ORIENTAL CHAIR, by the unanimous suffrages of their brethren, can be admitted to this degree of Masonry.

In its original establishment, when the temple of Jerusalem was finished, and the fraternity celebrated the capstone with great joy, it is demonstrable that none but those who had proved themselves to be complete masters of their profession, were admitted to this honor; and, indeed, the duties incumbent on every Mason, who is accepted and acknowledged as a Most Excellent Master, are such as render it indispensable that he should have a perfect knowledge of all the preceding degrees.

The following passage of Scripture is read at opening, accompanied by solemn ceremonies:

 The earth is the LORD's, and the fullness thereof; the world, and they that dwell therein. For he hath founded it upon the seas, and established it upon the floods Who shall ascend into the hill of the LORD? and who shall stand in his holy place? He that hath clean hands and a pure heart; who hath not lifted up his soul unto vanity, nor sworn deceitfully. He shall receive th blessing from the LORD, and righteousness from the GOD of his salvation. This is the generation of them that seek him, that seek thy face, O Jacob. Selah. Lift up your heads, O ye gates; and be ye lift up, ye everlasting doors; and the King of Glory shall come in Who is this King of Glory?

The LORD strong and mighty, the LORD mighty in battle. Lift up your heads, O ye gates; even lift them up ye everlasting doors; and the King of Glory shall come in. Who is this King of Glory The LORD of Hosts, he is the King of Glory. Selah.—PSALM xxiv.

* * * * * * * *

The following Psalm is read during the ceremony of receiving a candidate:

 l was glad when they said unto me, Let us go into the house of the Lord.— Our feet shall stand within thy gates, O Jerusalem. Jerusalem is builded as a city that is compact together: Whither the tribes go up, the tribes of the Lord, unto the testimony of Israel, to give thanks unto the name of the Lord. For there are set thrones of judgment, the thrones of the house of David. Pray for the peace of Jerusalem: they shall prosper that love thee. Peace be within thy walls, and prosperity within thy palaces. For my brethren and companions' sakes, I will now say, Peace be within thee. Because of the house of the LORD our GOD I will seek thy good."—Ps. cxxii.

* * * * * * * *

The following passages of scripture are also introduced, accompanied with solemn ceremonies :

Then said Solomon, The LORD
hath said that he would dwell
in the thick darkness. But
I have built an house of habitation for thee, and a place
for thy dwelling forever. And
the king turned his face, and
blessed the whole congregation of Israel : (and all
the congregation of Israel stood :) And he said,
Blessed be the LORD GOD of Israel, who hath with
his hands fulfilled that which he spake with his
mouth to my father David, saying, Since the day
that I brought forth my people out of the land of
Egypt, I chose no city among all the tribes of Israel
to build an house in, that my name might be there ;
neither chose I any man to be a ruler over my people Israel ; but I have chosen Jerusalem, that my
name might be there ; and have chosen David to be
over my people Israel. Now, it was in the heart
of David, my father, to build an house for the name
of the LORD GOD of Israel. But the LORD said to
David, my father, Forasmuch as it was in thine
heart to build an house for my name, thou didst
well in that it was in thine heart : notwithstanding,
thou shalt not build the house ; but thy son, which
shall come forth out of thy loins, he shall build the
house for my name. The LORD, therefore, hath
performed his word that he hath spoken ; for I am

risen up in the room of David, my father, and am set on the throne of Israel, as the Lord promised, and have built the house for the name of the Lord God of Israel; and in it have I put the ark, wherein is the covenant of the Lord, that he made with the children of Israel.

And he stood before the altar of the Lord, in the presence of all the congregation of Israel, and spread forth his hands: for Solomon had made a brazen scaffold of five cubits long, and five cubits broad, and three cubits high, and had set it in the midst of the court; and upon it he stood, and kneeled down upon his knees, before all the congregation of Israel, and spread forth his hands toward heaven, and said,

"O Lord God of Israel, there is no God like thee in heaven nor in the earth; which keepest covenant, and shewest mercy unto thy servants that walk before thee with all their hearts; thou which hast kept with thy servant David my father, that which thou hast promised him; and spakest with thy mouth, and hast fulfilled it with thine hand, as it is this day. Now, therefore, O Lord God of Israel, keep with thy servant David my father, that which thou hast promised him, saying, There shall not fail thee a man in my sight to sit upon the throne of Israel; yet so that thy children take heed

10

to their way to walk in my law, as thou hast walked before me. Now, then, O LORD GOD of Israel, let thy word be verified, which thou hast spoken unto thy servant David. But will GOD in very deed dwell with men on the earth? Behold, heaven and the heaven of heavens cannot contain thee; how much less this house which I have built! Have respect, therefore, to the prayer of thy servant, and to his supplication, O LORD my GOD, to hearken unto the cry and the prayer which thy servant prayeth before thee: that thine eyes may be open upon this house day and night, upon the place whereof thou hast said that thou wouldst put thy name there; to hearken unto the prayer which thy servant prayeth toward this place. Hearken, therefore, unto the supplications of thy servant, and of thy people Israel, which they shall make toward this place; hear thou from thy dwelling place, even from heaven; and, when thou hearest, forgive.

*   *   *   *   *   *   *   *

Now, my GOD, let, 1 beseech thee, let thine eyes be open; and let thine ears be attent unto the prayer that is made in this place. Now therefore arise, O LORD GOD, into thy resting-place, thou, and the ark of thy strength: let thy priests, O LORD GOD, be clothed with salvation, and let thy saints rejoice in goodness. O LORD GOD, turn not away the face of thine anointed: remember the mercies of David, thy servant.—II CHRON vi.

THE FOLLOWING ODE IS SUNG :

ALL hail to the morning
    That bids us rejoice ;
The temple 's completed,
    Exalt high each voice.
The capstone is finish'd,
    Our labor is o'er :
The sound of the gavel
    Shall hail us no more

To the Power Almighty, who ever has guided
    The tribes of old Israel, exalting their fame ;

To Him, who hath govern'd our hearts undivided,
  Let's send forth our voices to praise his great name.

        Companions, assemble
          On this joyful day ;
        (The occasion is glorious,)
          The keystone to lay ;
        Fulfill'd is the promise,
          By the ANCIENT OF DAYS,
        To bring forth the capstone
          With shouting and praise.

  *   *   *   *   *   *   *   *

There is no more occasion for level or plumb-line,
  For trowel or gavel, for compass or square ;
Our works are completed, the ARK safely seated,
  And we shall be greeted as workmen most rare

  *   *   *   *   *   *   *   *

        Now those that are worthy,
          Our toils who have shar'd,
        And prov'd themselves faithful,
          Shall meet their reward.
        Their virtue and knowledge,
          Industry and skill,
        Have our approbation,
          Have gained our good-will.

We accept and receive them, Most Excellent Masters
  Invested with honors, and power to preside ;
Among worthy craftsmen, wherever assembled.
  The knowledge of Masons to spread far and wide

ALMIGHTY JEHOVAH!
Descend now and fill
This lodge with thy glory,
Our hearts with good will!
Preside at our meetings,
Assist us to find
True pleasure in teaching
Good will to mankind.

Thy *wisdom* inspired the great institution,
Thy *strength* shall support it till nature expire;
And when the creation shall fall into ruin,
Its *beauty* shall rise through the midst of the fire.

Now when Solomon had made an end of praying the fire came down from heaven, and consumed the burnt-offering and the sacrifices; and the glory of the LORD filled the house. And the priests could not enter into the house of the LORD, because the glory of the LORD had filled the LORD's house. And when all the children of Israel saw how the fire came down, and the glory of the LORD upon the house, they bowed themselves with their faces to the ground upon the pavement, and worshipped, and praised the LORD, saying, FOR HE IS GOOD; FOR HIS MERCY ENDURETH FOREVER.—II CHRON.

THE FOLLOWING PSALM IS READ AT CLOSING:

 The LORD is my shepherd; I shall not want. He maketh me to lie down in green pastures; he leadeth me beside the still waters.—He restoreth my soul; he leadeth me in the paths of righteousness for his name's sake. Yea, though I walk through the valley of the shadow of death, I will fear no evil: for thou art with me; thy rod and thy staff they comfort me. Thou preparest a table before me, in the presence of mine enemies; thou anointest my head with oil; my cup runneth over. Surely goodness and mercy shall follow me all the days of my life; and I will dwell in the house of the LORD forever.—PSALM xxiii.

CHARGE TO THE CANDIDATE.

BROTHER :—Your admittance to this degree of
Masonry, is a proof of the good opinion the breth-
en of this lodge entertain of your masonic abilities
Let this consideration induce you to be careful of
forfeiting, by misconduct and inattention to our
rules, that esteem which has raised you to the rank
you now possess.

It is one of your great duties, as a Most Excellent
Master, to dispense light and truth to the unin-
formed Mason; and I need not remind you of the
impossibility of complying with this obligation
without possessing an accurate acquaintance with
the lectures of each degree.

If you are not already completely conversant in
all the degrees heretofore conferred on you, remember, that an indulgence, prompted by a belief that
you will apply yourself with double diligence to
make yourself so, has induced the brethren to accept you. Let it, therefore, be your unremitting
study to acquire such a degree of knowledge and
information, as shall enable you to discharge, with
propriety, the various duties incumbent on you, and
to preserve, unsullied, the title now conferred upon
you of a Most Excellent Master.

A Brief Description of King Solomon's Temple.

THIS structure, for beauty, magnificence and ex
pense, exceeded any building which was ever erected.
It was built of large stones of white marble, curiously hewn, and so artfully joined together, that
they appeared like one entire stone. Its inner walls,
beams, posts, doors, floors and ceilings, were made
of cedar and olive wood, and planks of fir, which
were entirely covered with plates of gold, with various beautiful engravings, and adorned with precious jewels of many colors. The nails which
fastened those plates were also of gold, with heads
of curious workmanship. The roof was of olive
wood, covered with gold, and when the sun shone
thereon, the reflection from it was of such a refulgent splendor that it dazzled the eyes of all who
beheld it. The court in which the temple stood,
and the courts without, were adorned on all sides
with stately buildings and cloisters ; and the gates
entering therein, were exquisitely beautiful and
elegant. The vessels consecrated to the perpetual
use of the temple, were suited to the magnificence
of the edifice in which they were deposited and
used.

Josephus states, that there were one hundred and
forty thousand of those vessels, which were made
of gold, and one million three hundred and forty

thousand of silver; ten thousand vestments for the priests, made of silk, with purple girdles; and two millions of purple vestments for the singers. There were also two hundred thousand trumpets, and forty thousand other musical instruments, made use of in the temple, and in worshipping GOD.

According to the most accurate computation of the number of talents of gold, silver and brass laid out upon the temple, the sum amounts to six thousand nine hundred and four millions, eight hundred and twenty-two thousand and five hundred pounds sterling; and the jewels are reckoned to exceed this sum. The gold vessels are estimated at five hundred and forty-five millions, two hundred and ninety-six thousand, two hundred and three pounds and four shillings sterling; and the silver ones at four hundred and thirty-nine millions, three hundred and forty-four thousand pounds sterling; amounting in all, to nine hundred and eighty-four millions, six hundred and thirty thousand, two hundred and thirty pounds, four shillings. In addition to this, there were expenses for workmen, and for materials brought from Mount Libanus and the quarries of Zeredatha. There were ten thousand men per month in Lebanon, employed in falling and preparing the timbers for the craftsmen to hew them; seventy thousand to carry burdens; eighty thousand to hew the stones and timber, and three thousand three hundred overseers of the work; who were all employed for seven years; to whom, besides their wages and diet, King Solomon gave, as a free gift, six millions, seven hundred and thirty-three thousand, nine hundred and seventy-seven pounds.

The treasure left by David, towards carrying on this noble and glorious work, is reckoned to be nine hundred and eleven millions, four hundred and sixteen thousand, two hundred and seven pounds ; to which, if we add King Solomon's annual revenue, his trading to Ophir for gold, and the presents made him by all the earth, we shall not wonder at his being able to carry on so stupendous a work ; nor can we, without impiety, question its surpassing all other structures, since we are assured that it was built by the immediate direction of HEAVEN

ROYAL ARCH.

LOSSING=BARRITT.

H I S degree is indescribably more august, sublime and important than all which precede it ; and is the summit and perfection of ancient Masonry. It impresses on our minds a belief of the being and existence of a Supreme Deity, without beginning of days or end of years ; and reminds us of the reverence due to his holy name. It also brings to light many essentials of the craft, which were, for the space of four hundred and seventy years, buried in darkness; and without a knowledge of which the Masonic character cannot be complete.

The lecture of this degree is divided into two sections, and should be well understood by every Royal Arch Mason; upon an accurate acquaintance with it, will depend his usefulness at our assemblies; and without it, he will be unqualified to perform the duties of the various stations in which his services may be required by the Chapter

SECTION I.

This section furnishes us with many interesting particulars relative to the state of the fraternity, during and since the reign of King Solomon; and illustrates the causes and consequences of some very important events which occurred during his reign. It explains the mode of government and organization of a Chapter; it designates the appellation, number and situation of the several officers, and points out the purposes and duties of their respective stations.*

---

* A Chapter of Royal Arch Masons consists of any convenient number of members, and the following officers, exclusive of the Treasurer, Chaplain, Stewards, and Tyler, viz: M. E. High Priest,—his station is in the East of the Sacred Sanctuary; E. King, in the East, on the right of the M. E. H. P.; E. Scribe, in the East, on the left of the M. E. H. P.; Captain of the Host, on the right, in front of the E. K.; Principal Sojourner, on the left, in front of the E. Scribe; Royal Arch Captain, within the Fourth Veil, or Sanctuary; M. of Third Veil, within the Third Veil; M. of Second Veil, within the Second Veil; M. of First Veil, within the First Veil

CHARGE AT OPENING

 Now we command you, brethren, that ye withdraw yourselves from every brother that walketh disorderly, and not after the tradition that ye received of us. For yourselves know how ye ought to follow us; for we behaved not ourselves disorderly among you Neither did we eat any man's bread for nought; but wrought with labor and travail night and day, that we might not be chargeable to any of you; not because we have not power, but to make ourselves an ensample unto you to follow us. For even when we were with you, this we commanded you, that if any would not work, neither should he eat. For we hear that there are some which walk among you disorderly, working not at all, but are busybodies. Now them that are such, we command and exhort, that with quietness they work, and eat their own bread. But ye, brethren, be not weary in well-doing. And if any man obey not our word by this epistle, note that man, and have no company with him, that he may be ashamed. Yet count him not as an enemy, but admonish him as a brother. Now the LORD of peace himself give you peace always by all means. The LORD be with you all.— II THESS. iii. 6–16.

＊　＊　＊　＊　＊　＊　＊　＊

SECTION II.

This section is fully supplied with illustrations of historical truth. It amplifies, in beautiful and striking colors, that prosperity and happiness are the sure attendants of perseverance and justice while dishonor and ruin invariably follow the practice of vice and immorality. It contains much that is beautifully illustrative of the preceding degrees ; a perfect knowledge of which is essential to the accomplished and well-informed Mason.

The following prayer, charges and passages of Scripture are introduced during the ceremony of Exaltation.

I will bring the blind by a way that they knew not ; I will lead them in paths that they have not known ; I will make darkness light before them, and crooked things straight. These things will I do unto them, and not forsake them.—Isa. xlii. 16

PRAYER.

" O thou eternal and omnipotent JEHOVAH, the glorious and everlasting I AM, permit us, thy frail, dependent and needy creatures, in the name of our *Most Excellent and Supreme High Priest*, to approach thy divine Majesty. And do thou, who

sittest *between the Cherubim*, incline thine ear to
the voice of our praises, and of our supplication;
and vouchsafe to commune with us from off the
mercy seat. We humbly adore and worship thy
unspeakable perfections, and thy unbounded goodness and benevolence. We bless thee, that when
man had sinned, and fallen from his innocence and
happiness, thou didst still leave unto him the powers of reasoning, and the capacity of improvement
and of pleasure. We adore Thee, that amidst the
pains and calamities of our present state, so many
means of refreshment and satisfaction are afforded
us, while traveling the *rugged path of life*. And
O, thou who didst aforetime appear unto thy servant
Moses, *in a flame of fire out of the midst of a
bush*, enkindle, we beseech thee, in each of our
hearts, a flame of devotion to thee, of love to each
other, and of benevolence and charity to all mankind. May the *veils* of ignorance and blindness be
removed from the eyes of our understandings, that
we may behold and adore thy mighty and wondrous
works. May the *rod* and staff of thy grace and
power continually support us, and defend us from
the rage of all our enemies, and especially from the
subtilty and malice of that old *serpent*, who with
cruel vigilance seeketh our ruin. May the *leprosy*
of sin be eradicated from our *bosoms;* and may
Holiness to the Lord be engraven upon all our
thoughts, words and actions. May the *incense* of
piety ascend continually unto thee, from off the

altar of our hearts, and *burn day and night*, as a sweet-smelling savor unto thee.   May we daily *search* the records of *truth*, that we may be more and more instructed in our duty ; and may we share the blessedness of those who hear the *sacred word* *and keep it*.   And finally, O merciful Father, when we shall have passed through the outward *veils* of these earthly *courts*, when the earthly house of this *tabernacle* shall be dissolved, may we be admitted into the *Holy of Holies* above, into the presence of the *Grand Council* of Heaven, where the Supreme *High Priest* forever presides. forever reigns."

Amen.   *So mote it be.*

*   *   *   *   *   *   *   *

Now Moses kept the flock of Jethro, his father-in-law, the priest of Midian ; and he led the flock to the back side of the desert, and came to the mountain of God, even to Horeb And the Angel of the Lord appeared unto him in a flame of fire, out of the midst of a bush ; and he looked, and behold, the bush burned with fire, and the bush was not consumed   And when the Lord saw that he turned aside to see, God called to him out of the midst of the bush, and said, Moses, Moses!   And he said, Here am I.   And he said, Draw not nigh hither : put off thy shoes from off thy feet. for the place whereon thou standest is holy ground.   Moreover, he said, I am the GOD of thy father, the GOD of Abraham, the GOD of Isaac, and the GOD of Jacob. And Moses hid his face, for he was afraid to look upon GOD."—EXOD. iii. 1–6.

* * * * * * * *

Zedekiah was one-and-twenty years old when he began to reign, and reign-ed eleven years in Jerusalem And he did that which was evil in the sight of the LORD his GOD and humbled not him self before Jeremiah th prophet speaking from the mouth of the LORD And he also rebelle against king Nebuchad nezzar, and stiffened his neck and hardened his heart, from turning unto the LORD GOD o Israel. Moreover, all the chie of the priests, and the people, transgressed ver much after all the abominations of the heathen and polluted the house of the LORD, which he ha hallowed in Jerusalem. And the LORD GOD o their fathers sent to them by his messengers, becaus he had compassion on his people and on his dwellin

place.   But they mocked the messengers of GOD and despised his words, and misused his prophets, until the wrath of the LORD arose against his people, till there was no remedy.   *   *   *   *   *   *
Therefore he brought upon them the king of the Chaldees, who slew their young men with the sword in the house of their sanctuary, and had no compassion upon young man or maiden, old man, o him that stooped for age ; he gave them all into his hand.   And all the vessels of the house of GOD, great and small, and the treasures of the house of the LORD, and the treasures of the king, and of his princes ; all these he brought to Babylon.   And they burnt the house of GOD, and brake down the wall of Jerusalem,   *   *   *   *   *   and burnt all the palaces thereof with fire, and destroyed all the goodly vessels thereof.   And them that had escaped from the sword, carried he away to Babylon ;— where they were servants to him and his sons, until the reign of the kingdom of Persia.—II CHRON xxxvi 11–20   *   *   *   *   *   *

Now, in the first year of Cyrus, king of Persia, the Lord stirred up the spirit of Cyrus, king of Persia, that he made a proclamation throughout all his kingdom, and put it also in writing, saying, Thus saith Cyrus, king of Persia, the LORD GOD of Heaven hath given me all the kingdoms of the earth, and he hath charged

me to build him an house at Jerusalem, which is in
Judah. * * * Who is there among you of all his
people ? his GOD be with him. and let him go up to
Jerusalem, which is in Judah, and build the house
of the LORD GOD of Israel, (he is the GOD) which
is in Jerusalem.—EZRA i. 1–3. * * * * * *

And Moses said unto GOD, Behold, when I come unto the children of Israel, and shall say unto
them, The GOD of your fathers
hath sent me unto you ; and they
shall say to me, What is his
name ? what shall I say unto
them ? And GOD said unto Moses, I AM THAT
I AM : And he said, Thus shalt thou say unto the
children of Israel, I AM hath sent me unto you.
EXODUS iii. 13, 14. * * * * * * * *

Lord, I cry unto thee : make haste unto me : give ear unto my voice Let my prayer be set before thee as an incense, and the lifting up of my hands as the evening sacrifice. Set a watch, O LORD, before my mouth ; keep the door of my lips. Incline not my heart to any evil thing, to practice wicked works with men that work iniquity. Let the righteous smite me, it shall be a kindness ; and let him reprove me, it shall be an excellent oil. Mine eyes are unto thee, O GOD the LORD ; in thee is my trust ; leave not my soul destitute. Keep me from the snare which they have laid for me, and the gins of the workers of iniquity. Let the wicked fall into their own nets, whilst that I withal escape.— PSALM cxli.

*   *   *   *   *   *   *   *

I cried unto the LORD with my voice ; with my voice unto the LORD did I make my supplication. I poured out my complaint before him: I shewed before him my trouble. When my spirit was overwhelmed within me, then thou knewest my path. In the way wherein I walked, have they privily laid a snare for me. I looked on my right hand and beheld, but there was no man that would know me: refuge failed me; no man cared for my soul. I cried unto thee, O Lord: I said, Thou art my refuge, and my portion in the land of the living. Attend unto my cry; for I am brought very low: deliver me from my persecutors; for they are stronger than I. Bring my soul out of prison, that I may praise thy name.—Psalm cxlii.

* * * * * * * *

Hear my prayer, O Lord, give ear to my supplications: in thy faithfulness answer me, and in thy righteousness. And enter not into judgment with thy servant; for in thy sight shall no man living be justified. For the enemy hath persecuted my soul; he hath smitten my life down to the ground; he hath made me to dwell in darkness. Therefore is my spirit overwhelmed within me; my heart within me is desolate. Hear me speedily, O Lord; my spirit faileth; hide not thy face from me, lest I be like unto them that go down into the pit. Cause me to hear thy loving kindness in the morning; for in thee do I trust cause me to know the way wherein I should walk for I lift up my soul unto thee. Teach me to do thy will; for thou art my God; bring my soul out of trouble, and of thy mercy cut off my enemies for I am thy servant.—Psalm cxliii.

* * * * * * * *

*   *   *   *   *   *   *   *

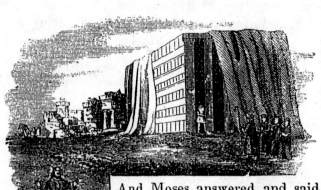

And Moses answered and said.
But, behold, they will not believe
me, nor hearken unto my voice;
for they will say, The LORD
hath not appeared unto thee
And the LORD said unto him, What is that in thine
hand? And he said, A rod. And he said, Cast it
on the ground. And he cast it on the ground, and
it became a serpent; and Moses fled from before it.
And the LORD said unto Moses, Put forth thine
hand, and take it by the tail. And he put forth
his hand, and caught it, and it became a rod in his
hand. That they may believe that the LORD GOD
of their fathers, the GOD of Abraham, the GOD of
Isaac, and the GOD of Jacob, hath appeared unto
thee.—EXODUS iv. 1–5.

*   *   *   *   *   *   *   *

And the LORD said furthermore unto him, Put now thy hand into thy bosom. And he put his hand into his bosom; and when he took it out, behold his hand was leprous as snow. And he said, Put thine hand into thy bosom again. And he put his hand into his bosom again; and plucked it out of his bosom, and behold, it was turned again as his other flesh. And it shall come to pass, if they will not believe thee, neither hearken to the voice of the first sign, that they will believe the voice of the latter sign.—EXODUS iv. 6–8

* * * * * * * *

And it shall come to pass, if they will not believe also these two signs, neither hearken unto thy voice, that thou shalt take of the water of the river, and pour it upon the dry land: and the water which thou takest out of the river, shall become blood upon the dry land.—EXODUS iv. 9

* * * * * * * *

Speak now to Zerubbabel, the son of Shealtiel, governor of Judah, and to Joshua, the son of Josedech, the high priest, and to the residue of the peo-

ple, saying, Who is left among you, that saw this house in her first glory? and how do ye see it now? is it not in your eyes in comparison of it as nothing? Yet now be strong, O Zerubbabel; and be strong, O Joshua, son of Josedech, the high priest; and be strong, all ye people of the land, for I am with you, saith the LORD of Hosts.

In that day will I take thee, O Zerubbabel, my servant, the son of Shealtiel, saith the LORD, and will make thee as a signet: for I have chosen thee.—HAGGAI ii. 2-23.

* * * * * * * *

The hands of Zerubbabel have laid the foundation of this house; his hands shall also finish it;  and thou shalt know that the LORD of Hosts hath sent me unto you. For who hath despised the day of small things? for they shall rejoice, and shall see the plummet in the hand of Zerubbabel with those seven.—ZECHARIAH iv. 9, 10.

* * * * * * * *

In that day will I raise up the tabernacle of David that is fallen, and close up the breaches thereof; and I will raise up his ruins, and I will build it as in the days of old.—AMOS ix. 11.

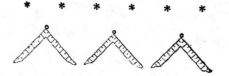

The following passages of scripture are read by the High Priest :

In the beginning GOD created the heaven and the earth. And the earth was without form, and void ; and darkness was upon the face of the deep ; and the Spirit of GOD moved upon the face of the waters. And GOD said, Let there be light ; and there was light.—GENESIS i. 1-3.

And it came to pass, when Moses had made an end of writing the words of this law in a book, until they were finished. that Moses commanded the Levites which bare the ark of the covenant of the Lord, saying, Take this book of the law, and put it in the side of the ark of the covenant of the LORD your GOD, that it may be there for a witness against thee.—DEUT. xxxi. 24-26.

And the LORD said unto Moses, Bring Aaron's rod again before the testimony, to be kept for a token.—NUMBERS xvii. 10.

And Moses said, This is the thing which the LORD commandeth, Fill an omer of the manna, to be kept for your generations; that they may see the bread wherewith I have fed you in the wilderness, when I brought you forth from the land of Egypt. And Moses said unto Aaron, Take a pot, and put an omer full of manna therein, and lay it up before the LORD, to be kept for your generations. As the Lord commanded Moses, so Aaron laid it up before the Testimony to be kept.—EXODUS xvi. 32–34.

* * * * * * * *

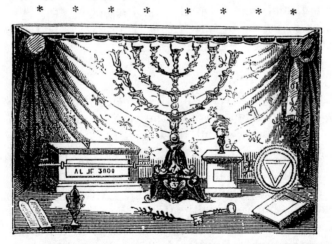

And thou shalt put the mercy-seat above, upon the ark; and in the ark thou shalt put the testimony that I shall give thee.—EXODUS xxv. 21.

For there was a tabernacle made; the first wherein was the candlestick, and the table, and the shew-bread; which is called the Sanctuary. And after the veils, the tabernacle, which is called the Holiest of all; which had the golden censer, and the ark of the covenant, overlaid round about with gold, wherein was the golden pot that had manna, and Aaron's rod that budded, and the tables of the covenant; and over it, the cherubims of glory shadowing the mercy-seat; of which we cannot now speak particularly.—HEBREWS ix. 2–5.

And GOD spake unto Moses, and said unto him, I am the Lord; and I appeared unto Abraham, unto Isaac, and unto Jacob, by the name of GOD ALMIGHTY; but by my name JEHOVAH was I not known to them.—EXODUS vi. 2–3.

*   *   *   *   *   *   *   *

The High Priest will then recite the following passage, previous to investing the candidate with an important secret of the degree:

In the beginning was the Word, and the Word was with GOD, and the Word was GOD. The same was in the beginning with GOD. All things were made by him: and without him was not anything made that was made. In him was life, and the life was the light of men. And the light shineth in darkness, and the darkness comprehended it not.—JOHN i 1–5.

The WORKING TOOLS of a Royal Arch Mason may be here explained.*

The working tools of a Royal Arch Mason, are the *Crow, Pickax* and *Spade.* The *Crow* is used by operative masons to raise things of great weight and bulk ; the *Pickax* to loosen the soil and prepare it for digging, and the *Spade* to remove rubbish. But the Royal Arch Mason is emblematically taught to use them for more noble purposes. By them he is reminded that it his sacred duty to lift from his mind the heavy weight of passions and prejudices, which incumber his progress towards virtue, loosening the hold which long habits of sin and folly have had upon his disposition, and removing the rubbish of vice and ignorance, which prevents him from beholding that eternal foundation of truth and wisdom upon which he is to erect the spiritual and moral temple of his second life.

CHARGE TO THE CANDIDATE.

WORTHY COMPANION : By the consent and assistance of the members of this Chapter, you are now exalted to the sublime and honorable degree of Royal Arch Mason. The rites and mysteries developed in this degree, have been handed down

---

* The symbolic character of the Masonic cabala ceasing with the Third Degree, it may not be deemed inappropriate to suggest the introduction of the above allegorical illustration as tending to beautify a "system of morality, veiled in allegory, and illustrated by symbols."

through a chosen few, unchanged by time, and uncontrolled by prejudice; and we expect and trust they will be regarded by you with the same veneration, and transmitted with the same scrupulous purity to your successors.

No one can reflect on the ceremonies of gaining admission into this place, without being forcibly struck with the important lessons which they teach. Here we are necessarily led to contemplate, with gratitude and admiration, the sacred Source from whence all earthly comforts flow. Here we find additional inducements to continue steadfast and immoveable in the discharge of our respective duties; and here we are bound by the most solemn ties, to promote each other's welfare, and correct each other's failings, by advice, admonition, and reproof. As it is our earnest desire, and a duty we owe to our companions of this order, that the admission of every candidate into this Chapter should be attended by the approbation of the most scrutinizing eye, we hope always to possess the satisfaction of finding none among us, but such as will promote, to the utmost of their power, the great end of our institution. By paying due attention to this determination, we expect your will never recommend any candidate to this Chapter, whose abilities, and knowledge of the preceding degrees you cannot freely vouch for, and whom you do not firmly and confidently believe, will fully conform to the principles of our order, and fulfill the obligations of a

Royal Arch Mason. While such are our members we may expect to be united in one object, without lukewarmness, inattention or neglect; but zeal, fidelity, and affection will be the distinguishing characteristics of our society; and that satisfaction, harmony and peace may be enjoyed at our meetings which no other society can afford.

CLOSING.

The Chapter is closed with solemn ceremonies; and the following prayer is rehearsed by the Most Excellent High Priest:

By the *Wisdom* of the Supreme High Priest, may we be directed; by his *Strength* may we be enabled, and by the *Beauty* of virtue may we be incited, to perform the obligations here enjoined on us; to keep inviolably the mysteries here unfolded to us; and invariably to practice all those duties out of the Chapter, which are inculcated in it."

Response—" So mote it be   Amen."

REMARKS RELATIVE TO KING SOLOMON'S TEMPLE

THIS famous fabric was situated on Mount Mo riah, near the place where Abraham was about to offer up his son Isaac, and where David met and appeased the destroying angel. It was begun in the fourth year of the reign of Solomon; the third after the death of David; four hundred and eighty

years after the passage of the Red Sea, and on the
second day of the month Zif, being the second
month of the sacred year, which answers to the
21st of April, in the year of the world, 2992 ; and
was carried on with such prodigious speed, that it
was finished, in all its parts, in li.tle more than seven
years.

By the Masonic art, and the wise regulations of
Solomon, every part of the building, whether of
stone, brick, timber or metal, was wrought and prepared before they were brought to Jerusalem ; so
that the only tools made use of in erecting the
fabric were wooden instruments prepared for that
purpose. The noise of the ax, the hammer, and
every other tool of metal, was confined to the forests
of Lebanon, where the timber was procured ; and
to Mount Libanus, and to the plains and quarries
of Zeredatha, where the stones were raised, squared,
marked and numbered ; that nothing might be
heard among the Masons at Jerusalem, but harmony and peace.

In the year of the world 3029, King Solomon died,
and was succeeded by his son Rehoboam, who, immediately after the death of his father, went down
to Shechem, where the chiefs of the people were met
together to proclaim him king.

When Jeroboam, the son of Nebat, who was in
Egypt, whither he had fled from the presence of Solomon, and whose ambition had long aspired to the
throne, heard of the death of the king, he hastened

to return from Egypt, to put himself at the head of
the discontented tribes, and lead them on to rebellion. He accordingly assembled them together.
and came to King Rehoboam, and spake to him
after this manner.

" Thy father made our yoke grievous ; now.
therefore, ease thou somewhat the grievous servi-
tude of thy father, and his heavy yoke that he put
upon us, and we will serve thee. And he said unto
them, Come again unto me, after three days. And
the people departed. And King Rehoboam took
counsel with the old men that had stood before
Solomon his father while he yet lived, saying, What
counsel give ye me, to return answer to this people ?
And they spake unto him saying, If thou be kind to
this people, and please them, and speak good words
to them, they will be thy servants forever. But he
forsook the counsel which the old men gave him,
and took counsel of the young men that were
brought up with him, that stood before him. And
he said unto them, what advice give ye, that we
may return answer to this people, which have spoken to me, saying, Ease somewhat the yoke that
hy father did put upon us ? And the young men
that were brought up with him spake unto him,
saying, Thus shalt thou answer the people that
spake unto thee saying, Thy father made our yoke
heavy, but make thou it somewhat lighter for us :
thus shalt thou say unto them, My little finger shall
be thicker than my father's loins. For, whereas

12

my father put a heavy yoke upon you, I will put more to your yoke; my father chastised you with whips, but I will chastise you with scorpions. So Jeroboam and all the people came to Rehoboam on the third day, as the king bade, saying, Come again to me on the third day. And the king answered them roughly, and King Rehoboam forsook the counsel o' the old men, and answered them after the advice of the young men, saying, My father made your yoke heavy, but I will add thereto; my father chastised you with whips, but I will chastise you with scorpions. And when all Israel saw that the king would not hearken unto them, the people answered the king, saying, What portion have we in David? and we have none inheritance in the son of Jesse: every man to your tents, O! Israel: and now, David, see to thine own house. So all Israel went to their tents."—II CHRON. x.

After a series of changes and events, of which an account may be found in the history of the Temple, Nebuchadnezzar, king of Babylon, with his forces, took possession of Jerusalem, and having made captive Jehoiachim, the king of Judah, elevated his uncle Zedekiah to the throne, after binding him by a solemn oath neither to make innovations in the government, nor to take part with the Egyptians in their wars against Babylon.

At the end of eight years, Zedekiah violated his oath to Nebuchadnezzar, by forming a treaty offensive and defensive with the Egyptians; thinking that jointly they could subdue the king of Babylon. Nebuchadnezzar immediately marched and ravaged Zedekiah's country, seized his castle and fortress, and proceeded to the siege of Jerusalem Pharaoh, learning how Zedekiah was pressed, advanced to his relief, with a view of raising the siege. Nebuchadnezzar, having intimation thereof, would not wait his approach, but proceeded to give him battle, and in one contest drove him out of Syria. This circumstance suspended the siege.

In the ninth year of Zedekiah's reign, the king of Babylon again besieged Jerusalem with a large army, and for a year and a half exerted all his strength to conquer it; but the city did not yield, though enfeebled by famine and pestilence.

In the eleventh year the siege went on vigorously; the Babylonians completed their works, having raised towers all around the city so as to drive the invaded party from the walls. The place, though a prey to plague and famine, was obstinately defended during the space of a year and a half. But at length, want of provisions and forces compelled its surrender, and it was accordingly delivered, at midnight, to the officers of Nebuchadnezzar.

In the seventieth year of the captivity of the Jews, and the first of the reign of Cyrus, king of Persia, he issued his famous edict purporting that the GOD adored by the Israelites, was the Eternal Being through whose bounty he enjoyed the regal dignity; and that he had found himself honorably mentioned by the prophets of ancient date, as the person who should cause Jerusalem to be rebuilt, and restore the Hebrews to their former state of grandeur and independency; he, therefore, gave orders for the release of the captives, with his permission to return to their own native country, to rebuild the city, and the house of the Lord.

The principal people of the tribes of Judah and Benjamin, with the priests and Levites, immediately departed for Jerusalem and commenced the undertaking; but many of the Jews determined to remain in Babylon, rather than relinquish the possessions they had obtained in that city.

The Jews who accepted the proposals of Cyrus, for rebuilding the city and temple, applied themselves with the greatest industry to prepare the foundations thereof, but had made no considerable progress when application was made by some of the neighboring nations, requesting the princes and governors, who had direction of the work, to prevent further proceedings. The most strenuous opposers of the intended structure were the Chuthites, who resided on the other side of the river, and whom Salmanezer, king of Assyria, had led to re-people Samaria, after he had expelled the Israelites.

During the year 3484, Joshua and Zerubbabel. incited by Haggai and Zechariah, go on with the work by order of Darius.

In the course of the year 3489, the second temple was completed.

ROYAL MASTER.

HIS degree is intimately connected with Royal Arch Masonry ; and cannot be conferred upon any one who has not
received the Royal Arch degree. It is short, but
contains much valuable information, and enables us
to comprehend those mysteries which are essentially necessary to a correct understanding of Royal
Arch Masonry

The following passages of Scripture are appropriate to this degree :

And Solomon made all the vessels that pertained unto the house of the LORD : the altar of gold, and the table of gold, whereupon the shewbread was ; and the candlesticks of pure gold ; five on the right side and five on the left, before the oracle ; with the flowers, and the lamps, and the tongs of gold ; and the bowls, and the snuffers, and the basins, and the spoons, and the censers, of pure gold ; and the hinges of gold, both for the doors of the inner house, the most holy place, and for the doors of the house, to wit, of the temple. So Hiram made an end of doing all the work that he made king Solomon for the house of the LORD.—1 KINGS vii. 48. 50. 40.

" And behold, I come quickly ; and my reward is with me, to give every man according as his work shall be. I am Alpha and Omega, the beginning and the end, the first and the last. Blessed are they that do his commandments, that they may have a right to the tree of life, and may enter in through the gates into the city.—REV. xxii. 12-14.

The officers, their titles and stations in a Council of Royal Masters, are as follows :

Most Illustrious Grand Master, as S., K. of I., in the East ; Right Illustrious Grand Master, H., K. of T., on the right of the M. I. G. M. ; Illustrious Conductor of the Work, (Adoniram, as Rep. of H. A.,) in the West ; Master of the Exchequer, as Treasurer, at the foot of the throne, on the right ; Recorder, at the foot of the throne, on the left ; Conducter of the Council, near the South ; Captain of the Guards, in the West, on the right ; Sentinel, at the Door.

And he set the cherubims within the inner house; and they stretched forth the wings of the cherubims, so that the wing of the one touched the one wall, and the wing of the other cherub touched the other wall; and their wings touched one another in the midst of the house.—I KINGS vi. 27.

The Ark, called the glory of Israel, which was seated in the middle of the holy place, under the wings of the cherubim, was a small chest or coffer, three feet nine inches long, two feet three inches wide, and three feet three inches high. It was made of wood, excepting only the mercy-seat, but overlaid with gold both inside and out. It had a ledge of gold surrounding it at the top, into which the cover, called the mercy-seat, was let in. The mercy-seat was of solid gold, the thickness of an hand's breadth; at the two ends were the two cherubim, looking inward towards each other, with their wings expanded, which, embracing the whole circumference of the mercy-seat, they met on each side, in the middle; all of the Rabbins say it was made out of the same mass, without any soldering of parts.

Here the *Schechina*, or Divine Presence rested, and was visible in the appearance of a cloud over it. From hence the Bathkoll issued, and gave answers when GOD was consulted. And hence it is, that GOD is said, in the Scripture, to dwell between the cherubim; that is, between the cherubim on the mercy-seat, because there was the seat or throne of the visible appearance of his glory among them.

SELECT MASTER.

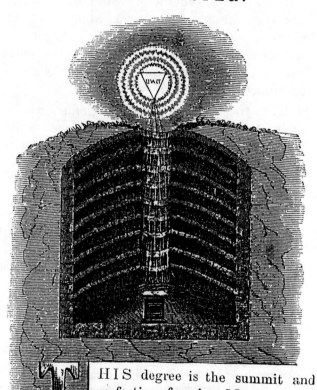

HIS degree is the summit and perfection of ancient Masonry; and without which the history of the Royal Arch Degree can hardly be said to be complete. It rationally accounts for the concealment and preservation of those essentials of the craft, which were brought to light at the erection of the second temple; and which lay concealed from the Masonic eye for four hundred and seventy years. Many particulars relative to those few who were selected, for their superior skill, to complete an important part of king Solomon's temple, are explained. And here, too, is exemplified an instance of *justice* and *mercy* by our ancient patron, towards one of the craft, who was led to disobey his commands by an *over-zealous* attachment for the institution. It ends with a description of a particular circumstance, which characterizes the degree.

PRAYER AT OPENING A COUNCIL.

May the Supreme Grand Master graciously preside over all our counsels, and direct us in all such things as he will be pleased to approve and bless. May our profession as Masons be the rule of our conduct as men. May our secret retreat ever continue to be the resort of the *just* and *merciful ;* the seat of the moral virtues, and the home of the *select. So mote it be.*

THE FOLLOWING PSALM IS READ :

His foundation is in the holy mountains. The LORD loveth the gates of Zion more than all the dwellings of Jacob. Glorious things are spoken of

---

The officers and stations of a Council of Select Masters are as follows:

Thrice Illustrious Grand Master, as K. S., in the East; Right Illustrious G. Master, as H., K. T., on the right, in the East. Illustrious G. Master, as H. A., (Principal Conductor of the Work,) on the left; Grand Treasurer; Grand Recorder; Grand Captain of the Guards, as Adoniram, in the West; Grand Conductor of the Council, as Azariah, in the South; Grand Marshal; Grand Steward, as Achizar, (Ahishar,) at the Door.

thee, O city of God. Selah. I will make mention of
Rahab and Babylon to them that know me. Behold
Philistia, and Tyre, with Ethiopia; this man was
born there. And of Zion it shall be said, This and
that man was born in her; and the Highest himself
shall establish her. The LORD shall count, when
he writeth up the people, that this man was born
there. Selah. As well the singers, as the players
on instruments, shall be there: all my springs are
in thee.—PSALM lxxxvii.

The following passages of Scripture are introduced and explained:

So king Solomon was king over all Israel. Azariah, the son of Nathan, was over the officers; and
Zabud, the son of Nathan, was principal officer,
and the king's friend; and Ahishar was over the
household; and Adoniram, the son of Abda, was
over the tribute.—I KINGS iv. 1–5–6.

 And the king commanded,
and they brought great stones,
costly stones, and hewed
stones, to lay the foundation
of the house. And Solomon's
builders and Hiram's builders
did hew them, and the stone-
squarers: so they prepared timber and stones to
build the house.—I Kings v. 17–18.

And king Solomon sent and fetched Hiram out
of Tyre. He was a widow's son, of the tribe of

Napthali ; and his father was a man of Tyre, a worker of brass ; and he was filled with wisdom and understanding, and cunning to work all works in brass.—I KINGS vii. 13–14.

The ancients of Gebal, and the wise men thereof, were in thee thy caulkers ; all the ships of the sea, with their mariners, were in thee, to occupy thy merchandise.''—EZEKIEL xxvii. 9.

And it came to pass, when Moses had made an end of writing the words of this law in a book, until they were finished, that Moses commanded the Levites which bare the ark of the covenant of the Lord, saying, Take this book of the law, and put it in the side of the ark of the covenant of the LORD your GOD, that it may be there for a witness against thee.—DEUT. xxxi. 24-26.

And Moses said, This is the thing which the LORD commandeth, Fill an omer of the manna, to be kept for your generations ; that they may see the bread wherewith I have fed you in the wilderness, when I brought you forth from the land of Egypt. And Moses said unto Aaron, Take a pot, and put an omer full of manna therein, and lay it up before the LORD, to be kept for your generations.   As the Lord commanded Moses, so Aaron laid it up before the Testimony to be kept.—EXODUS xvi. 32–34

 And the LORD said unto Moses, Bring Aaron's rod again before the testimony, to be kept for a token.—NUMBERS xvii. 10.

And when Moses was gone into the tabernacle of the congregation, to speak with him, then he heard the voice of one speaking to him from off the mercy-seat that was upon the ark of the testimony, from between the two cherubims: and he spake unto him.—NUMBERS vii. 89.

And look that thou make them after their pattern which was shewed thee in the mount.—EXODUS xxv 40.

------ • • ------

CHARGE TO THE CANDIDATE.

COMPANION :—Having attained to this degree you have passed the *circle of perfection* in ancient Masonry. In the capacity of Select Master you must be sensible that your obligations are increased in proportion to your privileges. Let it be your constant care to prove yourself worthy of the confidence reposed in you, and of the high honor conferred, in admitting you to this select degree. Let uprightness and integrity attend your steps; let *justice* and *mercy* mark your conduct; let *fervency* and *zeal* stimulate you in the discharge of the various duties incumbent upon you; but suffer not an dle or impertinent *curiosity* to lead you astray, or betray you into danger. Be *deaf* to every insinuation which would have a tendency to weaken your resolution, or tempt you to an act of *disobedience.* Be voluntarily *dumb* and *blind*, when the exercise of those faculties would endanger the peace of your mind, or the probity of your conduct; and let *silence* and *secrecy*, those cardinal virtues of a Select Master, on all necessary occasions, be scrupulously observed. By a steady adherence to the important instructions contained in this degree, you will merit the approbation of the select number with whom you are associated, and will enjoy the high satisfaction of having acted well your part in the important enterprise in which you are engaged; and, after having *wrought your regular hours*, may be admitted to participate in all the privileges of a *Select Master*.

CHARGE AT CLOSING.

COMPANIONS:—Being about to quit this sacred retreat, to mix again with the world, let us not forget, amid the cares and vicissitudes of active life, the bright example of sincere friendship, so beauti-

fully illustrated in the lives of the founders of this
degree.   Let us take the lesson home with us,
and may it strengthen the bands of fraternal love
between us; incite our hearts to duty, and our
desires to wisdom.   Let us exercise Charity, cherish
Hope, walk in Faith.   And may that moral principle, which is the mystic cement of our fellowship,
remain with and bless us.   *So mote it be.*

INSTALLATION CEREMONIES,

FOR COUNCILS OF ROYAL AND SELECT MASTERS.

1. The Most Puissant Grand Master of the Grand
Council, or his representative; or a Past Master of
a subordinate Council, will preside; and direct the
Recorder to read so much of the record as pertains
to the election of the officers.   After which he will
say:

2. " Companions of ——— Council—Do you remain satisfied with the choice you have made in the
selection of your officers for the ensuing year?"

3. The answer being in the affirmative, the officers
elect are arranged in due form; when the following
declaration is proposed:

"I, A—— B——, do solemnly promise, that I
will faithfully. and to the best of my ability, dis-

charge the duties of the office to which I have been elected; and that I will strictly conform to the requirements of the by-laws of this Council, and the regulations of the Grand Council, under which the same is holden, so far as they may come to my knowledge."

4. The Grand Marshal then presents the Thric Illustrious G. Master elect for installation, "as a companion well skilled in the Royal Mysteries; zealous in diffusing the select principles of our fathers, and in whose integrity and fidelity his brethren repose the highest confidence."

5. The installing officer then addresses him as follows:

THRICE ILLUSTRIOUS—I feel great satisfaction in receiving you as the Thrice Illustrious Master of this Council. It is a station highly honorable to him who diligently and faithfully performs the duties it devolves upon him. But previously to investing you with the appropriate jewel of your office, I must require your unequivocal assent to the following interrogatories;

I. Do you solemnly promise that you will use your utmost endeavors to correct the vices and purify the morals of your brethren; and to promote the peace, happiness and prosperity of your Council?

II. That you will not suffer your Select Council to be opened, when there are less than nine, or more than twenty-seven Select Masters present?

III. That you will not suffer any person to pass the circle of perfection in your Council, in whose integrity, fervency and zeal you have not entire confidence ?

IV. That you will not acknowledge or hold inter course with any Council that does not work under some regular and constitutional authority ?

V. That you will not admit any visitor into your Council who has not been regularly and lawfully invested with the degrees conferred therein, without his having previously been formally healed ?

VI. That you will faithfully observe and support such by-laws as may be made by your Council, in conformity with the Constitution and General Regulations of the Grand Council, under whose authority it works ?

VII. That you will pay due respect and obedience to the Grand Officers, when duly installed, and sustain them in the discharge of their lawful duties ?

VIII. Do you submit to all these requirements, and promise to observe and practice them faithfully?

Response : I Do.

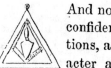 And now, Thrice Illustrious, with entire confidence in the rectitude of your inten tions, and in the integrity of your char acter as a Select Mason, I invest you with this jewel, the appropriate badge of your office

Having been honored with the free suffrages of your Companions, and elevated to the highest office

within their gift, it becomes your duty to set them
an example of diligence, industry and fidelity : to
see that the officers associated with you faithfully
perform their respective duties ; and that the interests and reputation of your Council are not endan-
gered by imprudence or neglect.

The important trust committed to your charge
will call forth your best exertions, and the exercise
of your best faculties. As the representative of the
wise King of Israel, it will be your duty to recite
the secret traditions, to illustrate the moral principles of the Order, to cherish the worthy, and hold
in due veneration the ancient landmarks.

By frequent recurrence to the by-laws of your
Council, and the general regulations of the fraternity, and a consistent observance of the great principles inculcated in the lectures and charges, you
will be enabled to fulfill the important obligations
resting upon you, with honor to yourself, and with
credit to the Craft. And may He, without whose
approving smiles our labors are all in vain, give
strength to your endeavors and support to your
exertions.

CHARGE TO THE RT. ILLUSTRIOUS GRAND MASTER.

COMPANION :—Having been elected to
the second office in this Council, it is
with pleasure that I invest you with
this jewel, the badge of your office.
The duties of the important office to which you

13

Companions have elevated you, will require your constant and earnest attention. You are to occupy the second seat in the Council; and it will be your duty to aid and support your chief in all the requirements of his office. In his absence, you will be called upon to preside in Council and to discharge his duties. Although the representative of a King, and elevated in rank above your Companions, may you never forget that, in all the duties you owe to GOD, your neighbor, and yourself, you and they stand upon the same level of equality. Let the bright example of your illustrious predecessor in the Grand Council at Jerusalem, stimulate you to the faithful performance of every duty; and when the King of Kings shall summon you to his immediate presence, from His hand may you receive a crown of glory, which shall never fade away.

CHARGE TO THE ILLUSTRIOUS GRAND-MASTER.

COMPANION:—As the third officer in the Council, I invest you with this badge. It is your duty to sound the Silver Trumpet at early dawn and eve of day, when the sun's first and last beams gild th mountain-tops; to announce high noon, and proclaim the time of rest and labor. In the absence of either of your superior officers, you will be required to perform his duties; and, as the interests of your Council ought never to be permitted to suffer through the want of intelligence in its officers.

you will allow me to urge upon you the necessity of being always qualified and prepared to meet such an emergency, should it ever arise. Having been admitted to the *fellowship of Kings*, you will be frequently reminded that the office of *mediator* is both honorable and praiseworthy. Let it, therefore, be your constant care to preserve harmony and unanimity of sentiment among the members of your Council. Discountenance whatever may tend to create division and dissension among the brethren in any of the departments of Masonry; and as the glorious sun at its meridian dispels the mists and clouds that obscure the horizon, so may your exertions tend to dissipate the mists of jealousy and discord, should they ever unfortunately arise in your Council

CHARGE TO THE GRAND TREASURER.

 COMPANION :—You have been elected to a responsible office, and I with pleasure invest you with this jewel. It is your duty to number and weigh out the Shekels of the Sanctuary, and to provide for the helpless orphan. The qualities which should distinguish you are accuracy and fidelity; accuracy in keeping a fair and true account of the receipts and disbursements; fidelity in carefully preserving the property and funds of the Council, and in rendering a just account of the same when required. Your interest in this Council, your attachment to the craft, and your known integrity of character, are a sure guaranty that your duties will be faithfully performed

CHARGE TO THE GRAND RECORDER.

COMPANION :—I now invest you with this badge of your office. The qualities which should recommend a Recorder are correctness in recording the proceedings o᾽ the Council; judgment in discriminating between what is proper and that which is improper to be written ; regularity in making the returns to the Grand Council; integrity in accounting for all moneys that may pass through his hands, and fidelity in paying the same over to the Grand Treasurer. The possession of these qualities has designated you as a suitable Companion for this important office ; and I entertain no doubt that you will discharge all the duties incumbent on you with fidelity aud honor. And when you shall have completed the record of your transactions here below, and finished the term of your probation, may you be admitted to the Grand Council above, and find your name recorded in the book of life eternal.

CHARGE TO THE G. CAPTAIN OF THE GUARDS.

COMPANION :—Having been elected Captain of the Guards, I present you with this implement of your office. Guard well your post, and suffer none to pass it but the select, the faithful and the worthy Be ever attentive to the commands of your chief and always near at hand to see them duly exe cuted

CHARGE TO THE GRAND CONDUCTOR.

COMPANION:—The office to which you have been elected is of much importance in the proceedings of the Council. I therefore invest you with this jewel. In the discharge of the duties you have voluntarily assumed, and with which you are familiar, be *fer vent* and *zealous*. Let uprightness and integrity attend your steps; let *justice* and *mercy* mark your conduct, and predominate in your heart through life.

CHARGE TO THE GRAND MARSHAL.

COMPANION:—The duties of your office require but little elucidation. It is your duty, in connection with the Conductor, to attend to the examination of visitors, and to take special care that none are permitted to enter but such as have proved their title to our favor and friendship. I present you with the implement of your office, in the confident belief that it is intrusted to competent and faithful hands.

CHARGE TO THE GRAND STEWARD.

COMPANION:—You are appointed Steward (or Sentinel) of this Council; and now invest you with this badge, and present you with this implement of your office. As the *Sword* is placed in the hands of the Steward to enable him to guard the Sanctuary and entrance to the *secret passage,* with sleepless vigilance, against *intruders,* so should it morally serve as a constant admonition to us to set a guard at the entrance of our thoughts; to place a watch at the door of our lips; to post a sentinel at the avenue of our actions; thereby excluding every unworthy thought, word and deed; and enabling us to preserve our consciences void of offence towards GOD and man.

CHARGE TO THE OFFICERS AND MEMBERS

COMPANIONS :—From the nature of the constitution of every society, some must *rule* and others *obey*. And while justice and moderation are required of the officers, in the discharge of their official duties, subordination and respect for their rulers are equally demanded of the members. The relation is reciprocal. The interests of both are inseparable; and, without mutual co-operation the labors of neither can succeed. Let the avenues to your passions be strictly guarded; let no curious intruder find his way into the secret recesses of your retirement, to disturb the harmony which should ever prevail among the select and chosen. In so doing, you will best secure the prosperity of your Council, the respect of your brethren, and the commendation of your own consciences.

The Grand Marshal will then proclaim the Council to be regularly constituted, and its officers duly installed.

ORDER OF HIGH PRIESTHOOD

H I S order appertains to the office of High Priest of a Royal Arch Chapter; and no one can be legally entitled to receive it, until he has been duly elected to preside as High Priest in a regular Chapter of Royal Arch Masons. This order should not be conferred when a less number than three duly qualified High Priests are present. Whenever the ceremony is performed in due and ample form, the assistance of at least nine High Priests, who have received it, is requisite

Though the High Priest of every regular Royal Arch Chapter, having himself been duly qualified, can confer the order under the preceding limitation as to number, yet it is desirable, when circumstances will permit, that it should be conferred by the Grand High Priest of the Grand Royal Arch Chapter, or such Present or Past High Priest as he may designate for that purpose. A convention, notified to meet at the time of any communication of the Grand Chapter, will afford the best opportunity of conferring this important and exalted degree of Masonry with appropriate solemnity. Whenever it is conferred, the following directions are to be observed :

A candidate desirous of receiving the order of High Priesthood, makes a written request to his predecessor in office, or, when it can be done, to the Grand High Priest, respectfully requesting that a convention of High Priests may be called, for the purpose of conferring on him the order. When the convention meets, and is duly organized, a certificate of the due election of the candidate to the office of High Priest must be produced. This certificate is signed by his predecessor in office, attested by the Secretary of the Chapter. On examination of this certificate, the qualifications of the candidate are ascertained. The solemn ceremonies of conferring the order upon him then ensue. When ended, the presiding officer directs the Secretary of the convention to make a record of the proceedings, and return it to the Secretary of the Grand Chapter, to be by him laid before the Grand High Priest, for the information of all whom it may concern. The convention of High Priests is then closed in due form

It is the duty of every companion, as soon after his election to the office of High Priest as is consistent with his personal convenience, to apply for admission to the order of High Priesthood, that he may be fully qualified properly to govern his Chapter.

The following passages of Scripture are made use of during the ceremonies appertaining to this order :

And they took Lot, Abram's brother's son, (who dwelt in Sodom,) and his goods, and departed. And there came one that had escaped, and told Abram the Hebrew ; for he dwelt in the plain of Mamre the Amorite, brother of Eshcol, and brother of Aner ; and these were confederate with Abram. And when Abram heard that his brother was taken captive, he armed his trained servants, born in his own house, three hundred and eighteen, and pursued them unto Dan. And he divided himself against them, he and his servants, by night, and smote them, and pursued them unto Hobah, which is on the left hand of Damascus. And he brought back all the goods, and also brought again his brother Lot, and his goods, and the women also, and the people. And the king of Sodom went out to meet him, after his return from the slaughter of Chedorlaomer, and of the kings that were with him, at the valley of Shevah, which is the king's dale. And Melchizedek, king of Salem, brought forth bread and wine: and he was the priest of the most high GOD. And he blessed him, and said, Blessed be Abram of the most high GOD, which hath delivered thine enemies into thy hand. And he gave him tithes of all. And the king of Sodom said unto Abram, Give me the persons, and take the goods to thyself. And Abram said to the king of Sodom, I have lifted up my hand unto the LORD, the most high GOD, the possessor of heaven and earth, that I will not take from a thread even to a shoe-latchet, and that I will not take anything that is thine, lest thou shouldst say, I have made Abram rich: save only that which the young men have eaten, and the portion of the men which went with me, Aner, Eshcol and Mamre ; let them take their portion.— GENESIS xiv. 12–24.

And the Lord spake unto Moses, saying, Speak unto Aaron, and unto his sons, saying, On this wise ye shall bless the children of Israel, saying unto them, the LORD bless thee, and keep thee ; the LORD make his face to shine upon thee, and be gracious unto thee ; the LORD lift up his countenance upon thee and give thee peace.—NUMB. vi. 22–26.

For this Melchisedec, king of Salem, priest of the most high GOD, who met Abraham returning from the slaughter of the kings, and blessed him; to whom also Abraham gave a tenth part of all, first being by interpretation, King of righteousness, and after that also, King of Salem, which is, King of peace; without father, without mother, without descent, having neither beginning of days, nor end of life, but made like unto the Son of GOD; abideth a priest continually. Now consider how great this man was, unto whom even the patriarch Abraham gave the tenth of the spoils. And verily, they that are of the sons of Levi, who receive the office of the priesthood, have a commandment to take tithes of the people according to the law, that is, of their brethren, though they come out of the loins of Abraham. For he testifieth, Thou art a priest forever after the order of Melchisedec. And inasmuch as not without an oath he was made priest. For those priests, (under the Levitical law) were made without an oath; but this with an oath, by him that said unto him, the LORD sware, and will not repent, Thou art a priest forever after the order of Melchisedec.—HEB. vii. 1–5–.17–20–21.

CEREMONIES AND CHARGES

UPON CONSTITUTING AND DEDICATING A ROYAL ARCH
CHAPTER AND INSTALLING ITS OFFICERS.

1. The Grand Officers will meet at a convenient place and open.

2. The subordinate Chapter will meet in the outer courts of their hall, and form an avenue for the reception of the Grand officers.

3. When formed, they will dispatch a Committee to the place where the Grand officers are assembled, to inform the Grand Marshal that the Chapter is prepared to receive them; the Grand Marshal will announce the committee, and introduce them to the Grand officers.

4. The Grand officers will move in procession, conducted by the committee, to the hall of the Chapter, in the following order:

GRAND MARSHAL

> Grand Tyler;
> Two Grand Stewards;
> Representatives of subordinate Chapters, according to seniority, by threes, triangular;
> Three Great Lights;
> Orator, Chaplain and other Clergy;
> Grand Secretary, Grand Treasurer, and Grand Royal Arch Captain;
> *Grand P. Sojourner, Grand Captain of the

---

* The Grand P. Sojourner, Grand Captain of the Host, and Grand Royal Arch Captain, are appointed pro tempore.

Host, and Deputy Grand High Priest;
Grand Scribe, Grand King, and Grand High Priest.

When the Grand High Priest enters the grand honors are given.

5. The Grand Secretary will then call over the names of the officers elect; and the Grand High Priest will ask whether they accept their respective offices. If they answer in the affirmative, he then asks the members whether they remain satisfied with their choice. If they answer in the affirmative, he directs their officers to approach the sacred volume, and become qualified for installation.

6. The Grand Marshal will then form the whole in procession, and they will march through the *veils* into the inner apartment, where they will surround the altar, which is previously prepared, in *ample form*, for the occasion.

7. All present will kneel, and the following prayer will be recited:

" Almighty and Supreme High Priest of heaven and earth! Who is there in heaven but thee, and who upon earth can stand in competition with thee? Thy OMNISCIENT mind brings all things in review, past, present and to come; thine OMNIPOTENT arm directs the movements of the vast creation; thine OMNIPRESENT eye pervades the secret recesses of every heart; thy boundless beneficence supplies us with every comfort and enjoyment; and thine unspeakable perfections and glory surpass the understanding of the children of men! Our Father, who art in heaven, we invoke thy benediction upon the purposes of our present assembly. Let this Chapter be established to thine honor : let its officers be endowed with wisdom to discern, and fidelity to pursue, its true interests ; let its members be ever mindful of the duty they owe to their GOD ; the obedience they owe to their superiors ; the love they owe to their equals, and the good will they owe to all mankind. Let this Chapter be consecrated to thy glory, and it members ever exemplify their love to GOD by their beneficence to man

Glory be to GOD on high.

Response—" So mote it be.   Amen."

The officers are then qualified in due form.

All the Companions, except High Priests and Past High Priests, are then desired to withdraw, while the new High Priest is solemnly bound to the performance of his duties ; and after the performance of other necessary ceremonies, not proper to be written, they are permitted to return.

8. The whole then return to their appropriate stations; when the Grand Marshal will form a general procession, in the following order:

Three Royal Arch Stewards with Rods ;
Tyler of a Blue Lodge ;
Entered Apprentices ;
Fellow Crafts ;

Master Masons;
Stewards of Lodges, having Jewels;
Deacons, having Jewels;
Secretaries, having Jewels;
Treasurers, having Jewels;
Wardens, having Jewels;
Mark Master Masons;
M. E. Masters;
Royal Arch Masons, by three;
Royal Masters, by three;
Select Masters, by three;
Orders of Knighthood;
Tyler of the new Chapter;
Members of the new Chapter, by three;
Three Masters of Veils;
Secretary, Treasurer, R. A. Captain; and
P. Sojourner, carrying the Ark;
A Companion, carrying the Pot of Incense;
Two Companions, carrying Lights;
Scribe, High Priest and King;
Grand Chapter, as before prescribed;

CAPTAIN OF THE HOST.

On arriving at the church, or house where the services are to be performed, they halt, open to the right and left, and face inward, while the Grand officers and others in succession, pass through and enter the house.

9. The officers and members of the new Chapter, and also of the Grand Chapter, being seated, the Grand Marshal proclaims silence, and the ceremonies commence.

10. An Anthem or Ode is to be performed.

11. An Oration or Address is to be delivered.

12. An Ode or piece of Music.

13. The Deputy Grand High Priest then rises and informs the Grand High Priest, that " a number of Companions, duly instructed in the sublime mysteries, being desirous of promoting the honor, and propagating the principles of the Art, have applied to the Grand Chapter for a warrant to constitute a new Chapter of Royal Arch Masons, which, having been obtained, they are now assembled for the purpose of being constituted, and having their officers installed in due and ancient form.

14. The Grand Marshal will then form the officers and members of the new Chapter in front of the Grand officers; after which, the Grand High Priest directs the Grand Secretary to read the warrant.

15. The Grand High Priest then rises and says, " By virtue of the high powers in me vested, I do form you, my respected Companions, into a regular Chapter of Royal Arch Masons. From henceforth you are authorised and empowered to open and hold a lodge of Mark Masters, Past Masters, and Most Excellent Masters, and a Chapter of Royal Arch Masons; and to do and perform all such things as thereunto may appertain; conforming, in all your doings, to the General Grand Royal Arch Constitution, and the general regulations of the State Grand

Chapter. And may the God of your fathers be with you, guide and direct you in all your doings."

16. The furniture, clothing, jewels, implements, utensils, etc., belonging to the Chapter, (having been previously placed in the centre, in front of the Grand officers, covered,) are now uncovered, and the new Chapter is dedicated in due and ancient form.

17. The dedication then follows: the Grand Chaplain saying,

"To our Most Excellent Patron, ZERUBBABEL, we solemnly dedicate this Chapter. May the blessing of our Heavenly High Priest descend and rest upon its members, and may their felicity be immortal.

"Glory be to GOD on high."—Response by the Companions.

"As it was in the beginning, is now, and ever hall be, world without end! Amen.—"So mote t be."

18. The Grand Marshal then says, "I am directed to proclaim, and I do hereby proclaim, this Chapter, by the name of —— Chapter,* duly consecrated, constituted and dedicated. This, etc.

19. An Ode.

----

* All legally constituted bodies of Royal Arch Masons are called Chapters; as regular bodies of Masons of the preceding degrees, are called Lodges. Every Chapter ought to assemble for work, at least once three months; and must consist of a High Priest, King, Scribe, Captain of the Host, Principal Sojourner, Royal Arch Captain, three Grand Masters of the Veils, Treasurer, Secretary, Tyler and as many members may be found convenient for working to advantage.

14

INSTALLATION.

20. The Deputy Grand High Priest will then present the first officer of the new Chapter to the Grand High Priest, saying,

" MOST EXCELLENT GRAND HIGH PRIEST :—I present you my worthy Companion —— ——, nominated in the warrant, to be installed High Priest of this (new) Chapter. I find him to be skillful in the royal art, and attentive to the moral precepts of our forefathers, and have therefore no doubt but he will discharge the duties of his office with fidelity.

The officers of the Chapter officiate in the lodges, holden for conferring the preparatory degrees, according to rank, as follows, viz :

The High Priest, as Master.
The King, as Senior Warden.
The Scribe, as Junior Warden.
The Captain of the Host, as Marshal or Master of Ceremonies.
The Principal Sojourner, as Senior Deacon.
The Royal Arch Chapter, as Junior Deacon.
The Master of the First Veil, as Junior Overseer.
The Master of the Second Veil, as Senior Overseer.
The Master of the Third Veil, as Master Overseer.
The Treasurer, Secretary, Chaplain, Stewards and Tyler, as officers of corresponding rank.

The High Priest of every Chapter has it in special charge, to see that the by-laws of his Chapter, as well as the General Grand Royal Arch Constitution, and all the regulations of the Grand Chapter, are duly observed ; that all the officers of his Chapter perform the duties of their respective offices faithfully, and are examples of diligence and industry to their companions ; that true and accurate records of all the proceedings of the Chapter are kept by the Secretary ; that the Treasurer keeps and renders exact and just accounts of all the moneys and other property belonging to the Chapter ; that the regular returns be made annually to the Grand Chapter ; and that the annual dues to the Grand Chapter be regularly and punctually paid. He has the right and authority of calling his chapter together at pleasure, upon any emergency or occurrence, which, in his judgment, may require their meeting. It is his privilege and duty, together with the King and Scribe, to attend the meetings of the Grand Chapter, either in person or by proxy ; and the well-being of the institution requires that this duty should on no occasion be omitted.

The Grand High Priest then addresses him as follows :

MOST EXCELLENT COMPANION.—I feel much satisfaction in performing my duty on the present occasion, by installing you into the office of High Priest of this (new) Chapter. It is an office highly honorable to all those who diligently perform the important duties annexed to it. Your reputed Masonic knowledge, however, precludes the necessity of a particular enumeration of those duties. I shall, therefore, only observe, that by a frequent recurrence to the constitution, and general regulations and constant practice of the several sublime lectures and charges, you will be best able to fulfill them ; and I am confident that the Companions who are chosen to preside with you, will give strength to your endeavors, and support your exertions. I shall now propose certain questions to you, relative to the duties of your office, and to which I must request your unequivocal answer.

I. Do you solemnly promise that you will redouble your endeavors to correct the vices, purify the morals, and promote the happiness of those of your Companions, who have attained this sublime degree ?

II. That you will never suffer your Chapter to be opened, unless there be present nine regular Royal Arch Masons ?

III. That you will never suffer either more or less than three brethren to be exalted in your Chapter at one and the same time?

IV. That you will not exalt any one to this degree, who has not shown a charitable and humane disposition; or who has not made a considerable proficiency in the foregoing degree?

V. That you will promote the general good of our order, and, on all proper occasions, be ready to give and receive instructions, and particularly from the General and State Grand officers?

VI. That to the utmost of your power, you will preserve the solemnities of our ceremonies, and behave, in open Chapter, with the most profound respect and reverence, as an example to your Companions?

VII. That you will not acknowledge or have intercourse with any Chapter that does not work under a constitutional warrant or dispensation?

VIII. That you will not admit any visitor into your Chapter, who has not been exalted in a Chapter legally constituted, without his being first formally healed?

IX. That you will observe and support such by-laws as may be made by your Chapter, in conformity to the General Grand Royal Arch Constitution, and the general regulations of the Grand Chapter?

X. That you will pay due respect and obedience to the instructions of the General and State Grand officers, particularly relating to the several lectures and charges, and will resign the chair to them, severally, when they may visit your Chapter?

XI. That you will support and observe the General Grand Royal Arch Constitution, and the general regulations of the Grand Royal Arch Chapter, under whose authority you act?

XII. That you will bind your successor in office to the observance of the same rules to which you have now assented?

Do you submit to all these things, and do you promise to observe and practice them faithfully?

These questions being answered in the affirmative, the Companions all kneel, and the Grand Chaplain repeats the following prayer:

"Most Holy and glorious LORD GOD, the Great High Priest of heaven and earth! we approach thee with reverence, and implore thy blessing on the Companion appointed to preside over this new assembly, and now prostrate before thee; fill his heart with thy fear, that his tongue and actions may pronounce thy glory. Make him steadfast in thy service; grant him firmness of mind; animate his heart, and strengthen his endeavors; may he teach thy judgments and thy laws; and may the incense he shall put before thee, upon thine altar, prove an acceptable sacrifice unto thee. Bless him, O LORD, and bless the work of his hands. Accept us, in mercy; hear thou from heaven, thy dwelling-place, and forgive our transgressions

Response—" So mote it be "

21. The Grand High Priest will then cause the High Priest elect to be invested with his clothing, badges, &c; after which he will address him as follows :

MOST EXCELLENT :—In consequence of your cheerful acquiescence with the charges, which you have heard recited, you are qualified for installation as the High Priest of this Royal Arch Chapter; and it is incumbent upon me, on this occasion, to point out some of the particulars appertaining to your office, duty and dignity.

The office of High Priest is a station highly honorable to all those who diligently perform the important duties annexed to it. By a frequent recurrence to the constitution and general regulations, and a constant practice of the several sublime lectures and charges, you will be best enabled to fulfill those duties; and I am confident that the Companions, who are chosen to preside with you, will give strength to your endeavors, and support to your exertions.

 Let the *mitre*, with which you are invested, remind you of the dignity of the office you sustain, and its inscription impress upon your mind a sense of your dependence upon GOD ; that perfection is not given unto man upon earth, and that perfect holiness belongeth alone unto the LORD.

The *breast-plate* with which you are decorated, in imitation of that upon which were engraven the names of the twelve tribes, and worn by the High Priest of Israel, is to teach you that you are always to bear in mind your responsibility to the laws and ordinances of the institution, and that the honor and interests of your Chapter and its members, should be always near your heart.

The *various colors* of the *robes* you wear, are emblematical of every grace and virtue which can adorn and beautify the human mind ; each of which will be briefly illustrated in the course of the charges to be delivered to your subordinate officers.

I now deliver into your hands the *Charter* under which you are to work ; you will receive it as a sacred deposit, and never permit it to be used for any other purposes than those expressed in it.

I present you with the *Book of the Law,* the great Light in every degree of Masonry. The doctrines contained in this sacred volume, create in us a belief in the dispensations of Divine Providence, which belief strengthens our FAITH, and enables us to ascend the first step of the Grand Masonic Ladder. This faith naturally produces in us a HOPE of becoming partakers of the promises expressed in this inestimable gift of GOD to man ; which hope enables us to ascend the second step. But the third and last being CHARITY, comprehends the former, and will continue to exert its influence, when Faith shall be lost in sight, and Hope in complete enjoyment.

I present you with the *Constitution* of the General Grand Royal Arch Chapter; the Rules and Regulations of the Grand Royal Arch Chapter of this State ; and also, with the *By-laws* of your Chapter. You will cause all these to be frequently read and punctually obeyed.

And now, Most Excellent, permit me, in behalf of the Craft here assembled, to offer you our most sincere congratulations on your accession to the honorable station you now fill. I doubt not you will govern with such order and regularity as to convince your Companions that their partiality has not been misplaced.

Companions of —— Chapter, — Behold your High Priest. [*They rise and bow, or, if the Installation be not public, salute him with the honors of Royal Arch Masonry.*] Recollect that the prosperity of your Chapter will as much depend on your support, assistance and obedience, as on his assiduity, information and wisdom.

22. The Marshal of the Chapter will then present the second officer to the Deputy Grand High Priest, who will present him to the Grand High Priest. The Grand High Priest will then ask him whether he has attended to the ancient charges and regulations before recited to his superior officer ; if he answers in the affirmative, he is asked whether

he fully and freely assents to the same: if he answers in the affirmative, the Grand High Priest directs his Deputy to invest him with his clothing, &c., and then addresses him as follows, viz:

CHARGE TO THE KING.

EXCELLENT COMPANION:—Th important station to which you are elected in this Chapter, requires from you exemplary conduct; its duties demand your most assiduous attention; you are to second and support your chief in all the requirements of his office; and should casualties at any time prevent his attendance, you are to succeed him in the performance of his duties. Your badge (the *Level*, surmounted by a *Crown*) should remind you, that although you are the representative of a King, and exalted by office above your companions, yet that you remain upon a level with them, as respects your duty to GOD, your neighbor, and yourself; that you are equally bound with them to be obedient to the laws and ordinances of the institution, to be charitable, humane and just, and to seek every oc¹ casion of doing good.

Your office teaches a striking lesson of humility. The institutions of political society teach us to consider the king as the chief of created beings, and that the first duty of his subjects is to obey his mandates:—but the institutions of our sublime degrees, by placing the King in a situation subordinate to the High Priest, teaches us that our duty to God is paramount to all other duties, and should ever claim the priority of our obedience to man; and that, however strongly we may be bound to obey the laws of civil society, yet that those laws, to be just, should never intermeddle with matters of conscience, nor dictate articles of faith.

The *Scarlet Robe*, an emblem of imperial dignity, should remind you of the paternal concern you should ever feel for the welfare of your Chapter, and the *fervency* and *zeal* with which you should endeavor to promote its prosperity.

In presenting to you the *Crown*, which is an emblem of royalty, I would remind you that, to reign sovereign in the hearts and affections of men, must be far more grateful to a generous and benevolent mind than to rule over their lives and fortunes; and that to enable you to enjoy this pre-eminence with honor and satisfaction, you must subject your own passions and prejudices to the dominion of reason and charity

You are entitled to the second seat in the council of your companions. Let the bright example of your illustrious predecessor in the Grand Council at Jerusalem, stimulate you to the faithful discharge of your duties; and when the King of kings shall summon you into his immediate presence, from his hand may you receive a *crown of glory*, which shall never fade away.

CHARGE TO THE SCRIBE.

 EXCELLENT COMPANION:—The office of Scribe, to which you are elected, is very important and respectable. In the absence of your superior officers, you are bound to succeed them and perform their duties. The purposes of the institution ought never to suffer for want of intelligence in its proper officers; you will therefore perceive the necessity there is of your possessing such qualifications as will enable you to accomplish those duties which are incumbent upon you, in your appropriate station, as well as those which may occasionally devolve on you by the absence of your superiors.

The *Purple Robe*, with which you are invested, is an emblem of *union*, and is calculated to remind you that the harmony and unanimity of the Chapter should be your constant aim; and to this end you are studiously to avoid all occasions of giving offence, or countenancing anything that may create divisions or dissensions. You are, by all means in your power, to endeavor to establish a permanent union and good understanding among all orders and degrees of masonry; and, as the glorious sun, at its meridian height, dispels the mists and clouds which obscure the horizon, so may your exertions tend to dissipate the gloom of jealousy and discord whenever they may appear.

Your badge (a *Plum-rule*, surmounted by a *Turban*,) is an emblem of rectitude and vigilance; and while you stand as a watchman upon the tower, to guard your companions against the approach of those enemies of human felicity, *intemperance* and *excess*, let this faithful monitor ever remind you to walk uprightly in your station; admonishing and animating your companions to fidelity and industry while at labor, and to temperance and moderation while at refreshment. And when the great Watchman of Israel, whose eye never slumbers nor sleeps, shall relieve you from your post on earth, may he permit you, in heaven, to participate in that food and refreshment which is

> " Such as the saints in glory love,
> And such as angels eat."

CHARGE TO THE CAPTAIN OF THE HOST.

 Companion: — The office with which you are entrusted is of high importance, and demands your most zealous consideration. The preservation of the most essential traits of our ancient customs usages and landmarks, are within your province; and it is indispensably necessary that the part assigned to you, in the immediate practice of our rites and ceremonies, should be perfectly understood and correctly administered.

Your office corresponds with that of *Marshal*, or Master of Ceremonies. You are to superintend all processions of your Chapter, when moving as a distinct body, either in public or private ; and as the world can only judge of our private discipline by our public deportment, you will be careful that the utmost order and decorum be observed on all such occasions. You will ever be attentive to the commands of your chief, and always near at hand to see them duly executed. I invest you with the badge of your office, and presume that you will give to your duties all that study and attention which their importance demands.

CHARGE TO THE PRINCIPAL SOJOURNER.

COMPANION :—The office confided to you, though subordinate in degree, is equal in importance to any in the Chapter, that of your chief alone excepted. Your office corresponds with that of *Senior Deacon*, in the preparatory degrees. Among the duties required of you, the preparation and introduction of candidates are not the least. As in our intercourse with the world, experience teaches that first impressions are often the most durable, and the most difficult to eradicate ; so it is of great importance, in all cases, that those impressions should be correct and just ; hence it is essential that the officer, who brings the blind by a way that they knew not, and leads them in paths that they have not known, should always be well qualified to make darkness light before them, and crooked things straight.

Your *robe of office* is an emblem of humility ; and teaches that, in the prosecution of a laudable undertaking, we should never decline taking any part that may be assigned us, although it may be the most difficult or dangerous.

The *rose-colored tesselated border*, adorning the robe, is an emblem of ardor and perseverance, and signifies, that when we have engaged in a virtuous course, notwithstanding all the impediments, hardships and trials we may be destined to encounter, should endure them all with fortitude, and ardently persevere unto the end ; resting assured of receiving, at the termination of our labors, a noble and glorious reward. Your past exertions will be considered as a pledge of your future assiduity in the faithful discharge of your duties.

CHARGE TO THE ROYAL ARCH CAPTAIN.

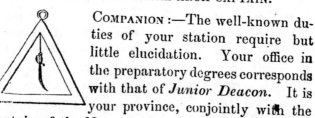

Companion :—The well-known duties of your station require but little elucidation. Your office in the preparatory degrees corresponds with that of *Junior Deacon*. It is your province, conjointly with the Captain of the Host, to attend the examination of all visitors, and to take care that none are permitted to enter the Chapter but such as have *traveled the rugged path* of trial, and evinced their title to our favor and friendship. You will be attentive to obey the commands of the Captain of the Host during the *introduction of strangers* among the workmen; and should they be permitted to pass your post, may they, by him, be introduced into the presence of the Grand Council.

The *White Banner*, intrusted to your care, is emblematical of that purity of heart and rectitude of conduct, which ought to actuate all those who pass the white veil of the sanctuary. I give it to you strongly in charge, never to suffer any one to pass your post without the *Signet of Truth*. I present you the badge of your office, in expectation of your performing your duties with intelligence, assiduity and propriety

CHARGE TO THE MASTER OF THE THIRD VEIL

COMPANION:—I present you with the *Scarlet Banner*, which is the ensign of your office, and with a sword to protect and defend the same. The rich and beautiful color of your banner is emblematical of *fervency* and *zeal*; it is the appropriate color of the Royal Arch degree. It admonishes us that we should be fervent in the exercise of our devotions to GOD, and zealous in our endeavors to promote the happiness of man.

CHARGE TO THE MASTER OF THE SECOND VEIL.

COMPANION:—I invest you with the *purple banner*, which is the ensign of your office, and arm you with a sword, to enable you to maintain its honor. The color of your banner is produced by a due mixture of *blue* and *scarlet;* the former of which is the characteristic color of the *symbolic* or *first three degrees of masonry*, and the latter that of the *Royal Arch degree*. It is an emblem of *union*, and is the characteristic color of the intermediate degrees. It admonishes us to cultivate and improve that spirit of union and harmony, between the brethren of the symbolic degrees, and the companions of the sublime degrees, which should ever distinguish the members of a society founded upon the principles of everlasting truth and universal philanthropy

CHARGE TO THE MASTER OF THE FIRST VEIL.

COMPANION:—I invest you with the *blue banner*, which is the ensign of your office, and a sword for its defence and protection. The color of your banner is one of the most durable and beautiful in nature. It is the appropriate color adopted and worn by our ancient brethren of the three symbolic degrees, and is the *peculiar characteristic* of an institution which has stood the test of ages, and which is as much distinguished by the durability of its materials or principles, as by the beauty of its superstructure.

is an emblem of universal *friendship* and benevlence; and instructs us that in the mind of a Mason those virtues should be as expansive as the lue arch of heaven itself.

CHARGE TO THE THREE MASTERS OF THE VEILS, AS OVERSEERS

COMPANIONS :—Those who are placed as overseers of any work should be well qualified to judge of its beauties and deformities, its excellencies and defects; they should be capable of estimating the former and amending the latter. This consideration should induce you to cultivate and improve all those qualifications with which you are already endowed, as well as to persevere in your endeavors to acquire those in which you are deficient. Let the various *colors* of the *banners* committed to your charge, admonish you to the exercise of the several virtues of which they are emblematic; and you are to enjoin the practice of those virtues upon all who shall present themselves, or the *work* of their hands *for* your *inspection*. Let no work receive your approbation but such as is calculated to adorn and strengthen the masonic edifice. Be industrious and faithful in practicing and disseminating a knowledge of the *true and perfect work*, which alone can stand the test of the *Grand Overseer's square,* in the

15

great day of trial and retribution.   Then, although
every *rod* should become a *serpent,* and every serpent an enemy to this institution, yet shall their
utmost exertions to destroy its reputation, or sap its
foundation, become as impotent as the *leprous hand,*
or as *water spilled upon the ground,* which cannot
be gathered up again.

CHARGE TO THE SECRETARY

COMPANION :—I with pleasure invest you with your badge as Secretary of this Chapter.   The
qualities which should recommend
a Secretary are, *promptitude* in
issuing the notifications and orders
of his superior officers; *punctuality* in attending
the meetings of the Chapter; *correctness* in recording their proceedings; *judgment* in discriminating
between what is proper and what is improper to be
committed to writing; *regularity* in making his
annual returns to the Grand Chapter; *integrity* in
accounting for all moneys that may pass through
his hands; and *fidelity* in paying the same over
into the hands of the Treasurer.   The possession of
these good qualities, I presume, has designated you
a suitable candidate for this important office; and
I cannot entertain a doubt that you will discharge
its duties beneficially to the Chapter, and honorably
to yourself.   And when you shall have completed the
record of your transactions here below, and finished

the term of your probation, may you be admitted into the celestial Grand Chapter of saints and angels, and and your name *recorded* in the *book of life eternal.*

CHARGE TO THE TREASURER.

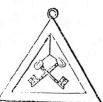

COMPANION : — You are elected Treasurer of this Chapter, and I have the pleasure of investing you with the badge of your office. The qualities which should recommend a Treasurer, are *accuracy* and *fidelity* ; accuracy in keeping a fair and minute account of all receipts and disbursements ; fidelity in carefully preserving all the property and funds of the Chapter, that may be placed in his hands, and rendering a just account of the same, whenever he is called upon for that purpose. I presume that your respect fo tne institution, your attachment to the interests of your Chapter, and your regard for a good name, which is better than precious ointment, will prompt you to the faithful discharge of the duties of your office.

CHARGE TO THE CHAPLAIN.

E. AND REV. COMPANION :—You are appointed Chaplain of this Chapter; and I now invest you with this jewel, the badge of your office. It is emblematical of eternity, and reminds us that here is not our abiding place. Your inclination will un

doubtedly conspire with your duty, when you perform, in the Chapter, those solemn services which
created beings should constantly render to their
infinite CREATOR; and which, when offered by one
whose holy profession is, "to point to heaven and
lead the way," may, by refining our morals,
strengthening our virtues, and purifying our minds,
prepare us for admission into the society of those
above, whose happiness will be as endless as it is
perfect

CHARGE TO THE STEWARDS.

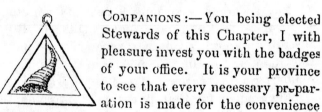

COMPANIONS:—You being elected
Stewards of this Chapter, I with
pleasure invest you with the badges
of your office. It is your province
to see that every necessary preparation is made for the convenience
and accommodation of the Chapter, previous to
the time appointed for meeting. You are to see
that the clothing, implements and furniture of each
degree, respectively, are properly disposed and in
suitable array for use, whenever they may be required, and that they are secured, and proper care
taken of them, when the business of the Chapter is
over. You are to see that necessary refreshments
are provided, and that all your companions, and particularly visitors, are suitably accommodated and
supplied. You are to be frugal and prudent in
your disbursements, and to be careful that no ex-

travagance or waste is committed in your department; and when you have faithfully fulfilled your stewardship here below, may you receive from heaven the happy greeting of "Well done, good and faithful servants."

CHARGE TO THE TYLER.

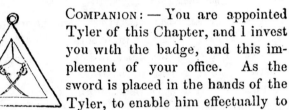

COMPANION: — You are appointed Tyler of this Chapter, and I invest you with the badge, and this implement of your office. As the sword is placed in the hands of the Tyler, to enable him effectually to guard against the approach of all *cowans and eaves-droppers*, and suffer none to pass or repass but such as are duly qualified; so it should morally serve as a constant admonition to us to set a guard at the entrance of our thoughts; to place a watch at the door of our lips; to post a sentinel at the avenue of our actions; thereby excluding every unqualified and unworthy thought, word and deed; and preserving consciences void of offence toward GOD and toward man.

As the first application from visitors for admission into the Chapter is generally made to the Tyler at the door, your station will often present you to the observation of strangers; it is therefore essentially necessary that he who sustains the office with which you are intrusted, should be a man of good morals, steady habits, strict discipline, temperate, affable and discreet. I trust that a just regard for the honor and reputation of the institution will ever induce you to perform, with fidelity, the trust reposed in you ; and when the door of this earthly tabernacle shall be closed, may you find an abundant entrance through the gates into the temple and city of our GOD.

ADDRESS TO THE HIGH PRIEST.

M. E. COMPANION:—Having been honored with the free suffrages of the members of this Chapter, you are elected to the most important office which is within their power to bestow. This expression of their esteem and respect should draw from you corresponding sensations: and your demeanor should be such as to repay the honor they have so conspicuously conferred upon you, by an honorable and faithful discharge of the duties of your office. The station you are called to fill is important, not only as it respects the correct practice of our rites and ceremonies, and the internal economy of the Chapter over which you preside; but the public reputation of the institution will be generally found to rise or fall according to the skill, fidelity and discretion with which its concerns are managed, and in proportion as the characters and conduct of its principal officers are estimable or censurable.

You have accepted a trust, to which is attached a weight of responsibility, that will require all your efforts to discharge, honorably to yourself and satisfactorily to the Chapter. You are to see that your officers are capable and faithful in the exercise of their offices. Should they lack ability you are expected to supply their defects; you are to watch carefully the progress of their performances, and to see that the long-established customs of the institution suffer no derangement in their hands. You are to have a careful eye over the general conduct of the Chapter; see that due order and subordination are observed on all occasions; that the members are properly instructed; that due solemnity be observed in the practice of our rites; that no improper levity be permitted at any time, but more especially at the *introduction of strangers among the workmen*

In fine, you are to be an example to your officers and members which they need not hesitate to follow; thus securing to yourself the favor of heaven and the applause of your brethren and companions

ADDRESS TO THE OFFICERS GENERALLY.

COMPANIONS IN OFFICE :—Precept and example should ever advance with equal pace. Those moral duties which you are required to teach unto others, you should never neglect to practice yourselves. Do you desire that the demeanor of your equals and inferiors toward you should be marked with deference and respect; be sure that you omit no opportunity of furnishing them with examples in your own conduct towards your superiors. Do you desire to obtain instruction from those who are more wise or better informed than yourselves ? Be sure that you are always ready to impart of your knowledge to those within your sphere, who stand in need of and are entitled to receive it. Do you desire distinction among your companions ? Be sure that your claims to preferment are founded upon superior attainments ; let no ambitious passion be suffered to induce you to envy or supplant a companion who may be considered as better qualified for promotion than yourselves ; but rather let a laudable emulation induce you to strive to excel each other in improvement and discipline ; ever remembering, that he who faithfully performs his duty, even in a subordinate or private station, is as justly entitled to esteem and respect, as he who is invested with supreme authority.

ADDRESS TO THE CHAPTER AT LARGE.

COMPANIONS :—The exercise and management of the sublime degrees of Masonry in your Chapter hitherto, are so highly appreciated, and the good reputation of the Chapter so well established, that I must presume these considerations alone, were there no others of greater magnitude, would be sufficient to induce you to preserve and to perpetuate this valuable and honorable character. But when to this is added the pleasure which every philanthropic heart must feel in doing good, in promoting good order ; in diffusing light and knowledge ; in cultivating Masonic and Christian charity, which are the great objects of this sublime institution, I cannot doubt that your future conduct, and that of your successors, will be calculated still to increase the lustre of your justly esteemed reputation.

May your *Chapter* become *beautiful* as the TEM PLE, *peaceful* as the ARK, and *sacred* as its *most holy place*. May your oblations of *piety* and *praise* be *grateful* as the INCENSE ; your love *warm* as its *flame*, and your charity diffusive as its fragrance. May your hearts be *pure* as the ALTAR, and your conduct *acceptable* as the OFFERING. May the exercise of your CHARITY be as constant as the returning wants of the distressed *widow* and helpless *orphan*. May the approbation of Heaven be your encouragement, and the testimony of a good conscience your support ; may you be endowed with every good and perfect gift, while *traveling the rugged path of life*, and finally be *admitted within the veil* of heaven, to the full enjoyment of life eternal. So mote it be Amen.

34. The officers and members of the Chapter will then pass in review in front of the grand officers, with their hands crossed on their breasts, bowing as they pass.

35. The Grand Marshal will then proclaim the Chapter, by the name of ———, Chapter No. —— to be regularly constituted, and its officers duly installed.

36. The ceremonies conclude with an Ode, or appropriate piece of music.

37. The procession is then formed, when they return to the place from whence they set out.

38. When the Grand officers retire, the Chapter will form an avenue for them to pass through, and salute them with the grand honors.

ENCAMPMENT DEGREES.

KNIGHTS OF THE RED CROSS.

THE Orders of Knighthood are conferred under the sanction of, or in connection with, Masonic assemblies. This degree is intimately associated with the Royal Arch, and cannot be conferred upon any brother who has not been exalted to that sublime degree.

It is founded upon incidents which occurred during the reign of DARIUS, king of Persia, and illustrates the difficulties and interruptions encountered by the

Jews in rebuilding the house of the LORD at Jerusalem

PRAYER AT OPENING.

O thou eternal, immortal and invisible GOD, who didst aforetime lead the children of Israel from the land of Egypt and out of the house of bondage; we would desire to come into thy presence, at thi time, with grateful hearts, to render thanks and praise for the wonderful display of thy goodness and mercy. Be thou pleased, O GOD, to be with thy servants who are now assembled in thy name; lift upon each one of us the light of thy countenance; defend us from the evil intentions of our enemies, while traveling the journey of life; and when we shall finally come into thy presence to be freed from the chains of sin and the sackcloth of repentance, be thou merciful unto us, O GOD, not according to our deserts, but according to our necessities; and thine shall be the praise forever and ever

---

TITLES, STATIONS, AND DECORATIONS.

Sovereign Master, upon a throne, in the East; Chancellor, on the right of the S. M.; Master of the Palace, on the left of the S. M.; Prelate, on the right of the C.; Master of Cavalry, on the right of the first division, when separately formed, and on the right of the whole, when formed in line; Master of Infantry, on the right of the second division, when separately formed, and on the left of the whole, when formed in line; Master of Finances, on the right, in front of the C.; Master of Despatches, on the left, in front of the M. of P.; Standard Bearer, in the West Sword Bearer, on the right of the St. B.; Warder, on the left of the St. B.; Guards, at the Passes; Sentinel, at the Door, outside. The knights are arranged, in equal numbers, on the right and left of the throne.

The assembly is denominated a Council. The drapery of the throne is green, a green banner is suspended above the throne; on it a triple triangle, with a red cross in the centre of each; underneath are arranged the emblems of the Order. The presiding officer wears a green collar, trimmed with red, to which is suspended a triple triangle. The knights wear a green collar, trimmed with red, and a sword and trowel, crosswise.

LESSON I.

The following passages of Scripture are appropriate to this order, and are rehearsed by the Prelate:

 " Now in the second year of their coming unto the house of GOD at Jerusalem, in the second month, began Zerubbabel, the son of Shealtiel, and Jeshua the son of Jozadak, and the remnant of their brethren the priests and the Levites, and all they that were come out of the captivity unto Jerusalem; and appointed the Levites, from twenty years old and upward, to set forward the work of the house of the LORD. Then stood Jeshua, with his sons and his brethren, Kadmiel and his sons, the sons of Judah, together to set forward the workmen in the house of God; the sons of Henadad, with their sons and their brethren the Levites. And when the builders laid the foundation of the temple of the Lord, they set the priests in their apparel with trumpets, and the Levites, the sons of Asaph, with cymbals, to praise the LORD, after the ordinance of David king of Israel. And they sang together by course, in praising and giving thanks unto the LORD: because he is good; for his mercy endureth forever toward Israel. And all the people shouted with a great shout when they praised the LORD, because the foundation of the house of the LORD was laid."

Now when the adversaries of Judah and Benjamin heard that the children of the captivity builded the temple unto the Lord God of Israel, then they came to Zerubbabel, and to the chief of the fathers, and said unto them, Let us build with you; for we seek your God as ye do; and we do sacrifice unto him, since the days of Esar-Haddon king of Assur, which brought us up hither. But Zerubbabel and Jeshua, and the rest of the chief of the fathers of Israel, said unto them, Ye have nothing to do with us to build an house unto our God; but we ourselves together will build unto the Lord God of Israel, as king Cyrus, the king of Persia, hath commanded us. Then the people of the land weakened the hands of the people of Judah, and troubled them in building; and hired counselors

against them, to frustrate their purpose, all the days of Cyrus, king of Persia even until the reign of Darius, king of Persia. And in the reign of Ahasuerus, in the beginning of his reign, wrote they unto him an accusation against the inhabitants of Judah and Jeru-

salem.   And in the days of Artaxerxes wrote Bish-
lam, Mithredath, Tabeel, and the rest of their companions, unto Artaxerxes king of Persia; and the
writing of the letter was written in the Syrian
tongue, and interpreting in the Syrian tongue.
Rehum the chancellor, and Shimshai the scribe.
wrote a letter against Jerusalem to Artaxerxes the
king, in this sort: this is the copy of the letter that
they sent unto him, even unto Artaxerxes the king:
Thy servants, the men on this side the river, and at
such a time.   Be it known unto the king, that the
Jews, which came up from thee to us, are come unto
Jerusalem, building the rebellious and the bad city,
and have set up the walls thereof, and joined the
foundations.   Be it known now unto the king, that
if this city be builded, and the walls set up again,
then will they not pay toll, tribute and custom, and
so thou shalt endamage the revenue of the kings
Now because we have maintenance from the king's
palace, and it was not meet for us to see the king's
dishonor; therefore have we sent and certified the
king: that search may be made in the book of the
records of thy fathers: so shalt thou find in the book
of the record, and know that this city is a rebellious
city, and hurtful unto kings and provinces, and that
they have moved sedition within the same of old
time: for which cause was this city destroyed.   We
certify the king, that if this city be builded again.
and the walls thereof set up, by this means thou
shalt have no portion on this side the river.   Then

sent the king an answer unto Rehum the chancellor, and to Shimshai the scribe, and to the rest of their companions that dwell in Samaria, and unto the rest beyond the river, Peace, and at such a time. The letter which ye sent unto us hath been plainly read before me. And I commanded, and search hath been made, and it is found that this city of old time hath made insurrection against kings, and that rebellion and sedition have been made therein. There have been mighty kings also over Jerusalem, which have ruled over all countries beyond the river; and toll, tribute and custom was paid unto them. Give ye now commandment to cause these men to cease, and that this city be not builded, until another commandment shall be given from me. Take heed now, that ye fail not to do this: why should damage grow to the hurt of the kings? Now, when the copy of king Artaxerxes' letter was read before Rehum, and Shimshai the scribe, and their companions, they went up in haste to Jerusalem, unto the Jews, and made them to cease by force and power. Then ceased the work of the house of GOD, which is at Jerusalem. So it ceased unto the second year of the reign of Darius, king of Persia.—EZRA iv.

LESSON II.

Darius the king, having ascended the throne of Persia, the children of the captivity were inspired with new hopes of protection and support in com-

leting their noble and glorious undertaking, which
ad been so often and so long impeded by their ad-
ersaries on the other side of the river.

The ancient historians inform us, that Darius,
hilst he was yet a private man, made a vow to
OD, that if he ever came to the throne he would
store all the holy vessels that were at Babylon,
d send them back again to Jerusalem.
Zerubbabel, one of the most excellent and faith-
l rulers of the Jews, having been formerly distin-
ished by the favorable notice and friendship of
e king, whilst in private life, offered himself to
counter the hazardous enterprise of traversing the
rsian dominions, and seeking admission to the

royal presence, in order that he might seize the first
favorable moment to remind the king of the vow
which he had made, and to impress upon his mind
the almighty force and importance of TRUTH.
From the known piety of the king no doubt was
entertained of obtaining his consent, that their enemies might be removed far from thence, and that
they might be no longer impeded in the glorious
undertaking in which they were engaged. The
council of rulers accepted, with great joy, this noble
sacrifice on the part of Zerubbabel, and invested
him with the necessary passports and commenda-
tions to enable him to pass through their own
dominions in safety. Having passed the barriers,
and entered the Persian dominions, he was taken
captive, clothed in the habiliments of a slave, and
put in chains : but not discouraged by this misfor-
tune, he declared himself a prince of the power of
Judah, and demanded an audience of the sovereign
He was told that he could only appear in the
presence of the sovereign as a captive and slave : to
which he consented, being impressed with a belief,
that if by any means he could gain access to the
king, he should succeed in the object of his journey

Zerubbabel, having thus gained admission to
the royal presence, was recognized by the king as
the friend and companion of his youth, and was
interrogated as to his motives in attempting to pass
the barriers of his dominions ; to which Zerubbabel
replied, that he was induced to seek the face of the

king by the tears and complaints of his brethren
and companions in Jerusalem, who were impeded,
by their adversaries on the other side of the river,
in the noble and glorious undertaking of rebuilding
the house of the LORD, in which they had been
permitted to engage by their late sovereign master,
Cyrus, the king; that this great work having been
made to cease by force and power, he had come to
implore the sovereign that he might be restored to
his confidence, and admitted amongst the servants
of his household. The king answered, that he had
often reflected, with peculiar pleasure, upon their
former intimacy; that he had heard, with great
satisfaction, of his fame as a wise and accomplished
ruler among the *architects* of his country; that
having a profound veneration for an institution

which was reputed to practise mysteries which were calculated to promote the glory of the nation, and the happiness of the people, he would instantly restore him to favor, upon condition that he would reveal those mysteries which so eminently distinguished the architects of the Jews from those of all other nations.

Zerubbabel replied, that their institution inculcated the doctrine that TRUTH is a divine attribute, and the foundation of every virtue; that to be good men and true was the first lesson they were taught; that his engagements were inviolable; that if he could obtain the royal favor only by the sacrifice of his integrity, he should humbly beg leave to renounce the protection of the sovereign, and cheerfully submit to an honorable exile, or a glorious death.

The king, struck with admiration at the firmness and discretion of Zerubbabel, declared that his virtue and integrity were truly commendable; that his fidelity to his engagements were worthy of imitation, and from that moment he was restored to his confidence.

Darius, in the first year of his reign, gave a splendid and magnificent entertainment to the princes and nobility; and after they had retired, finding himself unable to sleep, he fell into discourse with his three favorite officers, to whom he proposed certain questions, telling them, at the same time, that he who should give him the most reasonable and

satisfactory answer, should be clothed in purple, drink in a golden cup, wear a silken tiara, and a golden chain about his neck. He then proposed this question: which is greatest, the strength of WINE, of the KING, or of WOMEN? To this the first answered, *wine* is the strongest; the second, that the *king* was strongest; and the third, (who was Zerubbabel) that *women* were stronger, but above all things, TRUTH beareth the victory.

The king, being forcibly struck with the addition Zerubbabel had made to his question, ordered tha the princes and nobles should assemble on the fol lowing day, to hear the subject discussed.

LESSON III.

On the following day the king assembled together the princes and nobility, to hear the question de- bated. The first began as follows, upon

THE STRENGTH OF WINE.

"O ye princes and rulers, how exceeding strong is wine! it causeth all men to err that drink it; it maketh the mind of the king and the beggar to be all one; of the bondman and the freeman; of the poor man and of the rich; it turneth also every thought into jollity and mirth, so that a man remembereth neither sorrow nor debt; it changeth and elevateth the spirits, and enliveneth the heavy hearts of the miserable. It maketh a man forget his brethren, and draw his sword against his best friends. O ye princes and rulers, is not wine the strongest, that forceth us to do these things?"

Then began the second, and spoke as follows, upon

THE POWER OF THE KING.

"It is beyond dispute, O princes and rulers, that God has made man master of all things under the sun; to command them, to make use of them, and apply them to his service as he pleases: but whereas men have only dominion over other sublunary creatures, kings have an authority even over men themselves, and a right of ruling them by will and pleasure. Now, he that is master of those who are masters of all things else, hath no earthly thing bove him.'

Then began Zerubbabel, upon

THE POWER OF WOMEN AND OF TRUTH.

"O princes and rulers, the force of wine is not

to be denied; neither is that of kings, that unites so many men in one common bond of allegiance; but the supereminency of *woman* is yet above all this; for *kings* are but the gifts of women, and they are also the mothers of those that cultivate our *vineyards*. Women have the power to make us abandon our very country and relations, and many times to forget the best friends we have in the world, and, forsaking all other comforts, to live and die with them. But when all is said, neither they, nor wine, nor kings, are comparable to the almighty force of TRUTH. As for allother things, they are mortal and transient, but truth alone is unchangeable and everlasting; the benefits we receive from it are subject to no variations or vicissitudes of time and fortune. In her judgment is no unrighteousness, and she is the strength, wisdom, power and majesty of all ages. Blessed be the GOD of Truth."

When Zerubbabel had finished speaking, the princes and rulers cried out,

"Great is truth, and mighty above all things."

Then said the king to Zerubbabel, "Ask what thou wilt, and I will give it thee, because thou art found wisest among thy companions."

Then said he to Darius, "O king, remember thy vow, which thou hast vowed, to build Jerusalem in the day when thou shouldest come to thy kingdom, and to restore the holy vessels which were taken away out of Jerusalem. Thou hast also vowed to build up the temple, which was burned when Judah was made desolate by the Chaldees. And now, O king, this is that I desire of thee, that thou make good the vow, the performance whereof, with thine own mouth, thou hast vowed to the king of heaven."

Then Darius the king stood up and embraced him, and gave him passports and letters to his governors and officers, that they should safely convey both him, and those that should go with him, to Jerusalem; and that they should not be delayed or hindered from building the city and the temple until they should be finished. He also restored all the holy vessels remaining in his possession, that had been taken from Jerusalem, when the children of Israel were carried away captive to Babylon, and reserved by Cyrus.

LESSON IV.

But it came to pass, that when Sanballat, and Tobiah, and the Arabians, and the Ammonites, and the Ashdodites, heard that the walls of Jerusalem were made up, and hat the breaches began to be stopped, then they were very wroth, and conspired all of them together, to come and to fight against Jerusalem, and to hinder it. Nevertheless, we made our prayer unto our GOD, and set a watch against them day and night,

because of them.   And Judah said, The strength of the bearers of burdens is decayed, and there is much rubbish, so that we are not able to build the wall And our adversaries said, They shall not know, neither see, till we come in the midst among them, and slay them, and cause the work to cease.   And it came to pass, that when the Jews, which dwelt by them, came, they said unto us ten times, From all places whence ye shall return unto us, they will be upon you.   And it came to pass, when our enemies heard it was known unto us, and God had brought their counsel to naught, that we returned all of us to the wall, every one unto his work.   And it came to pass, from that time forth, that the half of my servants wrought in the work, and the other half of them held both the spears, the shields, and the bows, and the habergeons ; and the rulers were behind all the house of Judah.   They which builded on the wall, and they that bare burdens, with those that laded, every one with one of his hands wrought in the work, and with the other hand held a weapon.   For the builders, every one had his sword girded by his side, and so builded ; and he that sounded the trumpet was by me.   And I said unto the nobles, and to the rulers, and to the rest of the people, The work is great and large, and we are separated upon the wall, one far from another : In what place, therefore, ye hear the sound of the trumpet, resort ye thither unto us ; our GOD shall fight for us."—
NEHEMIAH iv. 7–20.

Then Darius the king made a decree, and search was made in the house of the rolls, where the treasures were laid up in Babylon. And there was found at Achmetha, in the palace that is in the province of the Medes, a roll, and therein was a record thus written : In the first year of Cyrus the king, the same Cyrus the king made a decree concerning the house of God at Jerusalem, Let the house be builded, the place, where they offered sacrifices, and let the foundations thereof be strongly laid ; the height thereof threescore cubits, and the breadth thereof threescore cubits ; with three rows of great stones, and a row of new timber ; and let the expenses be given out of the king's house. And also let the golden and silver vessels of the house of GOD, which Nebuchadnezzar took forth out of the temple which is at Jerusalem, and brought unto Babylon, be restored, and brought again unto the temple which is at Jerusalem, every one to his place, and place them in the house of God. Now, therefore, Tatnai, governor beyond the river, Shethar-boznai, and your companions, the Apharsachites, which are beyond the river, be ye far from thence : let the work of this house of GOD alone ; let the governor of the Jews, and the elders of the Jews, build this house of GOD in his place. Moreover, I make a decree what ye shall do to the elders of these Jews, for the building of this house of GOD ; that of the king's goods, even of the tribute beyond the river, forthwith expenses be given unto these men, that they be not hindered. And that which they have need of, both young bullocks, and rams, and lambs, for burnt-offerings of the GOD of heaven ; wheat, salt, wine and oil, according to the appointment of the priests which are at Jerusalem, let it be given them day by day without fail ; that they may offer sacrifices of sweet savors unto the GOD of heaven, and pray for the life of the king, and of his sons. Also, I have made a decree, that whosoever shall alter this word, let timber be pulled down from his house, and being set up let him be hanged thereon ; and let his house be made a dunghill for this. And the GOD that hath caused his name to dwell there destroy all kings and people, that shall put to their hand to alter and to destroy this house of GOD which is at Jerusalem. I Darius have made a decree ; let it be done with speed. Then Tatnai, governor on this side the river Shethar-boznai, and their companions, according to that which Darius the king had sent, so they did speedily. And the elders of the Jews builded, and they prospered through the prophesying of Haggai the prophet, and Zechariah, the son of Iddo ; and they builded and finished it, according to the commandment of the God of Israel, and according to the commandment of Cyrus, and Darius, and Artaxerxes, king of Persia.—EZRA vi.

KNIGHTS TEMPLARS.

H E Order of Knights of Malta, who were originally called Hospitallers of St. John of Jerusalem, took its rise about the year 1099; from which time, to the year 1118, their whole employment was works of charity, and taking care of the sick.

Some time after the establishment of this order, nine gentlemen formed a society to guard and protect the Christian pilgrims who traveled from abroad, to visit the Holy Sepulchre.

These men were encouraged by the Abbot of Jerusalem, who assigned them and their companions a place of retreat in a Christian church, called the church of the Holy Temple, from which they were called Templars.

PRAYER AT OPENING.

Supreme Architect of the Universe, whose All-Seeing Eye surveys the inhabitants of this lower world, behold us, thy dependent creatures, with thy favor and blessing. We adore thee as a holy and

---

DECORATIONS AND STATIONS OF OFFICERS.

The throne is situated in the East; above is suspended a banner, on it a cross irradiated with rays of light : on each side a sky-blue banner, on one of which are arranged the emblems of the Order, and on the other a Paschal lamb and Maltese cross, with the motto, "THE WILL OF GOD." The Most Eminent Grand Commander is seated on the throne, the Generalissimo, Prelate, and Past Grand Commanders on his right; the Captain General on his left; the Treasurer on the right, and the Recorder on the left in front : the Senior Warden at the south-west angle of the triangle, and upon the right of the first division; the Junior Warden at the north-west angle of the triangle, and on the left of the third division; the Standard Bearer in the west, the Sword Bearer on his right and the Warder on his left; Guards, at the Passes; Sentinel, at the Door, outside. The Knights are so arranged, that there shall be an equal number on each side of the throne and in front. Three tents, at proper distances, in an adjoining room, or in the north of the Encampment, and stationed in front, with a black banner, having a star of nine points; in the centre of the star, a cross and serpent of gold, surrounded by a circle, with the motto, "IN HOC SIGNO VINCES," painted upon it.

UNIFORM.

A full suit of black, with a sword and military hat; a black velvet sash, trimmed with silver lace, hanging on the right shoulder and crossing the body to the left side; at the end of the sash is suspended a poniard; on the left hip of the sash a Maltese cross is placed in the centre of a green rosette; on the right shoulder a black rosette and star; on the left breast a star of nine points; in the centre of the star, a cross and serpent of gold, surrounded by a circle, in which is engraved, "IN HOC SIGNO VINCES;" also, a Paschal lamb, with a flag, a cock, and red cross. On the flap of the apron three stars are placed in a triangular form, with cross swords in the centre; on the centre of the apron twelve knobs or stars placed in a triangle, with skull and cross bones in the centre.

merciful GOD, whose righteous providence orders all things in heaven and on earth; and from whom all holy desires, all good counsels, and all just works do proceed. We beseech thee to direct and bless us in what we do. Give us wisdom to choose, and grace to perform, whatever is according to thy holy will. Preserve us from every sin; protect us in every danger, and grant that all our doings, being ordered by thy governance, may be righteous in thy sight. Especially would we at this time render thee our thanksgiving and praise for the Institution, as members of which we are now assembled, and for all the pleasures we have derived from it. We thank thee that the few, who are here met together, have been favored with new inducements, and laid under new and stronger obligations to virtue and holiness. Endue us, O Lord, our Redeemer, with thy spirit, with wisdom and fortitude to resist the temptation of our unruly passions while traveling the pilgrimage of this life, so that, when solicited by avarice, we may not, with Judas, sell our GOD, or so far yield to the weakness and infirmities of our nature, as, with Peter, to deny our Master. But by the beauty of holiness, may we be incited to practice that charity which is recorded in thy Word, and so let our light shine before men, that they, seeing our good works, may glorify thee, our Father, which art in heaven. Grant this, O merciful God, through Him, who is the resurrection and the life, thy Son, our Savior, Jesus Christ. Amen

CHARGE AT OPENING.

James, a servant of God and of the Lord Jesus Christ, to the twelve tribes which are scattered abroad, greeting. My brethren, count it all joy when ye fall into divers temptations; knowing this, that the trying of your faith worketh patience. But let patience have her perfect work, that ye may be perfect and entire, wanting nothing. If any of you lack wisdom, let him ask of God, that giveth to all men liberally, and upbraideth not; and it shall be given him. But let him ask in faith, nothing wavering. For he that wavereth is like a wave of the sea, driven with the wind and tossed. For let not that man think that he shall receive anything of the Lord. A double-minded man is unstable in all his ways. Let the brother of low degree rejoice in that he is exalted. If any man among you seem to be religious, and bridleth not his tongue, but deceiveth his own heart, this man's religion is vain. Pure religion and undefiled before God and the Father is this : To visit the fatherless and widows in their affliction, and to keep himself unspotted from the world.—JAMES i. 1–10–26–27

LESSON I.

FIRST EXHORTATION

——— I greet thee.   *   *   *

Silver and gold have I none : but such as I have give I thee.   *   *   *   *   *   *

Hearken to a lesson to cheer thee on thy way, and assure thee of success.

And Abraham rose up early in the morning, and took bread and a bottle of water and gave it unto Hagar (putting it on her shoulder,) and the child, and sent her away, and she departed and wandered in the wilderness, and the water was spent in the bottle, and she cast the child under one of the shrubs ; and the angel of GOD called to Hager out of heaven, saying, Arise, lift up the lad, and hold him in thine hand ; for I will make him a great nation : and GOD opened her eyes, and she saw a well of water.

By faith Abraham sojourned in the land of promise, as in a strange country, dwelling in tabernacles; for he looked for a city which hath foundations. whose builder and maker is GOD.

Be ye therefore followers of GOD as dear children, rejoicing in the Lord always; and again I say, ejoice. Farewell—GOD speed thee.

SECOND EXHORTATION.

—— I greet thee.   *   *   *   *   *

If a brother or sister be naked and destitute of daily food, and one of you say, Depart in peace, be ye warmed and filled, and ye give them not of those things which are needful for the body, what doth it profit? To do good and to communicate, forget not, for with such sacrifices God is well pleased

Beware lest any man spoil you through philosophy and vain deceit, after the traditions of men; after the rudiments of the world, and not after Christ: For in him dwelleth all the fullness of the Godhead bodily.   Farewell—GOD speed thee.

THIRD EXHORTATION.

—— I greet thee.   *   *   *   *   *

He that receiveth you, receiveth me, and he that receiveth me, receiveth him that sent me. Come into me all ye that labor and are heavy laden, and i will give you rest. Take my yoke upon you and earn of me, for I am meek and lowly in heart, and 'e shall find rest unto your souls, for my yoke is

17

easy and my burden is light.   Whosoever shall give
to drink unto one of these little ones a cup of cold
water only, in the name of a disciple, verily I say
unto you he shall in no wise lose his reward.

Farewell—GOD speed thee.

LESSON II.

Then one of the twelve, called Judas Iscariot,
went unto the chief priests and said unto them, What

will ye give me, and I will
deliver him unto you. And
they covenanted with him
for thirty pieces of silver·
And from that time h
sought opportunity to be-
tray him. Now, the first day
of the feast of unleavened

bread, the disciples came to Jesus, saying unto him.

Where wilt thou that we prepare for thee to eat the passover? And he said, Go into the city to such a man, and say unto him, The Master saith, My time is at hand; I will keep the passover at thy house with my disciples. And the disciples did as Jesus had appointed them; and they made ready the passover. Now, when the even was come, he sat down with the twelve. And as they did eat, he said, Verily I say unto you, that one of you shall betray me. And they were exceeding sorrowful, and began every one of them to say unto him, Lord, is it I? And he answered and said, he that dippeth his hand with me in the dish, the same shall betray me. The Son of man goeth, as it is written of him; but wo unto that man by whom the Son of man is betrayed! It had been good for that man if he had not been born. Then Judas, which betrayed him, answered and said, Master, is it I? He said unto him, Thou hast said.—MATT. xxvi. 14–25.

* * * * * * * *

LESSON III.

Then cometh Jesus with them unto a place called Gethsemane, and saith unto the disciples, Sit ye here, while I go and pray yonder. And he took with him Peter and the two sons of Zebedee, and began to be sorrowful and very heavy. Then saith he unto them, My soul is exceeding sorrowful, even unto death, tarry ye here, and watch with me. And he went a little farther, and fell on his face, and prayed, saying, O my Father, if it be possible, let this cup pass from me; nevertheless, not as I will, but as thou wilt. And he cometh unto the disciples, and findeth them asleep, and saith unto Peter, What! could ye not watch with me one hour? Watch and pray, that ye enter not into temptation; the spirit indeed is willing, but the flesh is weak. He went away again the second time, and prayed, saying, O my Father, if this cup may not pass away from me, except I drink it, thy will be done. And he came and found them asleep again; for their eyes were heavy. And he left them, and went away again, and prayed the third time, saying the same words. Then cometh he unto his disciples. and saith unto them, Sleep on now, and take your rest: behold the hour is at hand, and the Son of man is betrayed into the hands of sinners. Rise, let us be going: behold, he is at

hand that doth betray me And while he yet spake, lo! Judas, one of the twelve, came, and with him a great multitude, with swords and staves, from the chief priests and elders of the people. Now he that betrayed him, gave them a sign, saying, Whomsoever I shall kiss, that same is he: hold him fast And forthwith he came to Jesus, and said, Hail, Master; and kissed him.—MATT xxvi. 36–50.

*   *   *   *   *   *   *

LESSON IV.

When Pilate saw that he could prevail nothing, but that rather a tumult was made, he took water, and washed his hands before the multitude, saying, I am innocent of the blood of this just person; see ye to it. Then answered all the people, and said, His blood be on us, and on our children. Then released he Barabbas unto them: and when he had scourged Jesus, he delivered him to be crucified. Then the soldiers of the governor took Jesus into the common hall, and gathered unto him the whole band of soldiers. And they stripped him, and put on him a scarlet robe. And when they had platted a crown of thorns they put it upon his head, and a reed in his right hand; and they bowed the knee before him, and mocked him, saying, Hail, king of the Jews! And they spit upon him, and took the reed and smote him on the head. And after that they had mocked him, they took the robe off from him, and put his own raiment on him, and led him away to crucify him. And as they came out, they found a man of Cyrene, Simon by name: him they compelled to bear his cross. And when they were come unto a place called Golgotha, that is to say, A place of a skull, they gave him vinegar to drink, mingled with gall: and when he had tasted thereof he would not drink. And they crucified him, and parted his garments, casting lots; that it might be fulfilled which was spoken by the prophet; They parted my garments among them, and upon my vesture did they cast lots. And sitting down, they watched him there; and set up over his head his accusation written, THIS IS JESUS THE KING OF THE JEWS.—MATT. xxvii. 24-37.

*   *   *   *   *   *   *   *

LESSON V.

Although it is appointed unto all men once to die, yet the Scriptures inform us, that the Savior of the world arose from the dead and ascended into heaven, there forever he is seated on the throne of majesty on high; and they also assure us, that all who have received Him for their righteousness, and put their trust in Him, shall rise to life everlasting.

In the end of the Sabbath, as it began to dawn, toward the first day of the week, came Mary Magdalene and the other Mary, to see the sepulchre. And behold there was a great earthquake for the angel of the Lord descended from heaven, and came and rolled back the stone from the door, and sat upon it. His countenance was like lightning, and his raiment white as snow: and for fear of him the keepers did shake, and became as dead men. And the angel answered and said unto the women, "Fear not ye: for I know that ye seek Jesus, which was crucified. He is not here ; for he is risen, as he said. Come, see the place where the Lord lay: and go quickly, and tell his disciples that he is risen from the dead ; and behold he goeth before you into Galilee ; there shall ye see him : lo! I have told you." And they departed quickly from the sepulchre, with fear and great joy, and did run to bring his disciples word.

And as they went to tell his disciples, behold Jesus met them, saying, All hail. And they came and held him by the feet, and worshipped him.

 And he led them out, as far as to Bethany ; and he lifted up his hands, and blessed them. And it came to pass, while he blessed them, he was parted from them, and carried up into heaven. And they worshipped him, and returned to Jerusalem with great joy.

* * * * * * * *

The following ode may be appropriately introduced during the ceremonies :

    The rising GOD forsakes the tomb !
      Up to his Father's court he flies ;
    Cherubic legions guard him home,
      And shout him welcome to the skies.

    Break off your tears, ye saints, and tell
      How high our great deliv'rer reigns,
    Sing how he spoil'd the hosts of hell,
      And led the monster, death, in chains

    Say live forever, wondrous king,
      Born to redeem, and strong to save,
    Then ask the tyrant, "where's thy sting ?
      And where's thy vict'ry, boasting grave ?"

   *   *   *   *   *   *   *   *

LESSON VI.

And in those days Peter
stood up in the midst of the
disciples, and said, (the
number of the names to-
gether were about an hun-
dred and twenty,) Men and
brethren, this scripture
must needs have been ful-
filled which the Holy Ghost,
by the mouth of David, spake before concerning
Judas, which was guide to them that took Jesus.
For he was numbered with us, and had obtained

rt of this ministry. Now this man purchased a
ld with the reward of iniquity; and falling head-
ng, he burst asunder in the midst, and all his
wels gushed out. And it was known unto all the
vellers at Jerusalem; insomuch as that field is
lled, in their proper tongue, Aceldama, that is
say, The field of blood. For it is written in
e book of Psalms, Let his habitation be desolate,
d let no man dwell therein: and his bishopric
t another take. Wherefore, of these men which
ve companied with us, all the time that the Lord
sus went in and out among us, beginning from
e baptism of John unto that same day that he
s taken up from us, must one be ordained to be
witness with us of his resurrection. And they
pointed two, Joseph called Barsabas, who was
rnamed Justus and Matthias. And they prayed
d said, Thou, Lord, which knowest the hearts of
l men, show whether of these two thou hast cho-
n, that he may take part of this ministry and
ostleship, from which Judas by transgression fell,
at he might go to his own place. And they gave
rth their lots; and the lot fell upon Matthias;
d he was numbered with the eleven apostles.—
cts i. 15–26

KNIGHTS OF MALTA.

THE Knights of St. John, or Hospitallers of St. John, afterward known as Knights of Rhodes, and finally called Knights of Malta, was a military religious Order, established at about the commencement of the Crusades. As early as 1048, some merchants from Amalfi, in Naples, being struck with the misery to which the pilgrims were exposed on their road to the Holy Land, obtained permission of the Caliph of Egypt, to erect a church and build a monastery near the site of the Holy Sepulchre at Jerusalem, which they dedicated to St. John the Baptist. They entertained all pilgrims that came for devotion, and cured the diseased among them. They became eminent for their devotion, charity and hospitality. St. John the Baptist, being their patron, they were called Brethren Hospitallers of St. John the Baptist of Jerusalem, to distinguish them from the Knights of the Holy Sepulchre. They took the black habit of the Hermits of St. Augustine, and on the left breast wore a cross of eight points. "In war they wore crimson, with a white cross, but in their monasteries, and on the day of their profession, the black garment only."

The following passages of Scripture are rehearsed in Encampments of Knights of Malta:

LESSON I.

And when they were escaped, then they knew that the island was called Melita. And the barbarous people showed us no little kindness; for they kindled a fire, and received us every one, because of the present rain, and because of the cold And when Paul had gathered a bundle of sticks, and laid them on the fire, there came a viper out of the heat, and fastened on his hand. And when the barbarians saw the venomous beast hang on his hand, they said among themselves, No doubt this man is a murderer, whom, though he hath escaped the sea, yet vengeance suffereth not to live And he shook off the beast into the fire, and felt no harm. Howbeit they looked when he should have swollen, or fallen down dead suddenly; but after they had looked a great while, and saw no harm come to him.—ACTS xxviii. 1-6.

LESSON II.

And Pilate wrote a title, and put it on the cross. And the writing was, JESUS OF NAZARETH, THE KING OF THE JEWS.—ST. JOHN xix. 19

LESSON III.

But Thomas, one of the twelve called Didymus, was not with them when Jesus came. The other disciples, therefore, said unto him, We have seen the Lord. But he said unto them, Except I shall see in his hands the prints of the nails, and put my finger into the print of the nails, and thrust my hand into his side, I will not believe. And after eight days, again his disciples were within, and Thomas with them. Then came Jesus, the doors being shut, and stood in the midst, and said, Peace be unto you. Then saith he to Thomas, Reach hither thy finger, and behold my hands; and reach hither thy hand, and thrust it into my side; and be not faithless, but believing. And Thomas answered, and said unto him, My Lord and my God.—ST. JOHN xx. 24-28.

CHARGE TO THE CANDIDATE.

SIR KNIGHT:—Having passed through the several degrees and honorary distinctions of our ancient and honorable institution—in your admission to the tesselated Masonic ground floor—your ascent into the middle chamber—your entrance to the unfinished sanctum sanctorum—your regularly passing the several gates of the temple—induction to the oriental chair—witnessing the completion and dedication of that superb model of excellence, the Temple, which has immortalized the names of our ancient Grand Masters, and the justly celebrated craftsmen:—having wrought in the ruins of the first Temple, and from its sacred Royal Arch brought to light incalculable treasures and advantages to the craft:—having duly studied into the way and manner of their concealment; also having been engaged in the hazardous enterprise of traversing an enemy's dominions, and there convincing a foreign prince that truth is great and will prevail; therefore, you are now admitted to a participation in those labors which are to effect the erection of a temple more glorious than the first, even that beauteous temple of holiness and innocence, whose pillars are Charity, Mercy and Justice, the foundation of which is in the breast of every one who has tasted that the Lord is gracious: to whom you come as unto a living stone, disallowed indeed of men, but chosen of God and precious.

And now, Sir Knight, we bid you welcome to all these rights and privileges, even to that disinterested friendship and unbounded hospitality which ever has, and we hope and trust ever will continue to adorn, distinguish and characterize this noble order

It will henceforth become your duty, and should be your desire, to assist, protect and befriend th weary way-worn traveler, who finds the heights of fortune inaccessible, and the thorny paths of life broken, adverse and forlorn,—to succor, defend and protect the innocent, the distressed and the helpless, ever standing forth as a champion to espouse the cause of the Christian religion.

You are to inculcate, enforce and practice virtue; and amidst all the temptations which surround you, never be drawn aside from the path of duty, or forgetful of those due guards and pass-words which are necessary to be had in perpetual remembrance; and while one hand is wielding the sword for your Companion in danger, let the other grasp the mystic Trowel, and widely diffuse the genuine cement of Brotherly Love and Friendship.

Should calumny assail the character of a brother Sir Knight, recollect that you are to step forth and vindicate his good name, and assist him on all necessary occasions. Should assailants ever attempt your honor, interest or happiness, remember, also, at the same time, you have the counsel and support of your brethren, whose mystic swords, combining the virtues of Faith, Hope and Charity, with Justice, Fortitude, and Mercy will leap from their scabbards in defence of your just rights, and insure you a glorious triumph over all your enemies.

On this occasion permit me, Sir Knight, to re mind you of our mutual engagements, our recipro cal ties; whatever may be your situation or rank in life you will find those, in similar stations, who have dignified themselves and been useful to mankind. You are therefore called upon to discharge all your duties with fidelity and patience, whether in the field, in the senate, on the bench, at the bar, or at the Holy Altar. Whether you are placed upon the highest pinnacle of worldly grandeur, or glide more securely in the humble vale of obscurity, unnoticed, save by a few; it matters not, for a few rolling suns will close the scene, when naught but holiness will serve as a sure pass-word to gain admission into that REST prepared from the foundation of the world.

If you see a brother bending under the cross of adversity and disappointment, look not idly on, neither pass by on the other side, but fly to his relief. If he be deceived, tell him the Truth; if he be calumniated, vindicate his cause; for, although in some instances, he may have erred, still recollect that indiscretion in him should never destroy humanity in you.

Finally, Sir, Knights, as *memento mori* is deeply engraved on all sublunary enjoyments, let us ever be found in the habiliments of righteousness, traversing the straight path of rectitude, virtue and true holiness, so that having discharged our duty here below, performed the pilgrimage of life, burst the bands of mortality, passed over the Jordan of death, and safely landed on the broad shore of eternity, there, in the presence of myriads of attending angels, we may be greeted as brethren, and received into the extended arms of the Blessed Immanuel, and forever made to participate in his Heavenly kingdom.

AN EXHORTATION AT CLOSING.

Finally, my brethren, be strong in the Lord, and in the power of his might. Put on the whole armor of GOD that ye may be able to stand against the wiles of the devil. For we wrestle not against flesh and blood, but against principalities, against powers, against the rulers of the darkness of this world, against spiritual wickedness in high places. Wherefore, take unto you the whole armor of GOD, that ye may be able to withstand in the evil day, and having done all, to stand. Stand, therefore, having your loins girt about with truth, and having on the breast-plate of righteousness; and your feet shod with the preparation of the gospel of peace; above all, taking the shield of faith, wherewith ye shall be able to quench all the fiery darts of the wicked. And take the helmet of salvation, and the sword of the Spirit, which is the Word of God.— EPHES. vi. 10–17

CEREMONIES AND CHARGES

UPON CONSTITUTING AND DEDICATING A COMMANDERY,
AND INSTALLING ITS OFFICERS.

———

The Sir Knights will assemble in the room where the ceremonies are to be performed, and open a Commandery. The jewels are then placed on the altar. An ode is then sung, succeeded by prayer.

The Grand Marshal will then say, " Right Eminent Grand Commander, a constitutional number of Knights Templar, duly instructed in the sublime mysteries of our Orders, and being desirous of promoting the honor of the same by aiding the cause of *humanity, knowledge* and *virtue*, have applied to proper authority for a warrant or charter to constitute them a regular Commandery of Knights Templar, and the appendant Orders. The prayer of their petition having been granted, they are now assembled for the purpose of being legally constituted, and of having their officers installed in due and ancient form."

The Grand Commander will then direct the Grand Recorder to read the charter, which being done, he will ask the members if they still approve of the officers named in the charter; if they assent, the Grand Commander will declare :

" By virtue of the high power and authority in me vested, I do now form you, my worthy brother knights,

18

into a just and regular Commandery of Knights Templar. Henceforth you are authorized and empowered to form and open a Council of Knights of the Red Cross, a Commandery of Knights Templar, and Knights of Malta, of the Order of St. John of Jerusalem, and to perform all such things as may appertain to the same; conforming in all your doings to the laws and constitution of the Grand Commandery, under whose authority you act, and to the constitution and edicts of the Grand Encampment of the United States. And may the God of your fathers be with you, guide and direct you in all your undertakings."

The jewels are now uncovered to solemn music, when the Prelate rises and says:

"From time immemorial, it has been customary for the Masonic fraternity to dedicate the different departments of our institution to different patrons. We dedicate our Lodges to Sts. John the Baptist, and the Evangelist; our Chapters to Zerubbabel, and our Commanderies to St. John the Almoner. We do this not in that superstitious sense in which the brethren employ the term when they set apart their temples for the worship of their imaginary deities, nor in that high and solemn sense in which Christians dedicate their churches to the great Jehovah; but we do it simply to testify our respect and esteem for the character of those who have been so eminently beneficial to our institution, and that their examples may stimulate us to imitate their exalted virtues.

"To our most eminent and worthy Patron St. John the Almoner, I do now solemnly dedicate this Commandery, by the name and title of ——— Commandery: and may the God of all grace abundantly bless you in your laudable undertaking, and may each one of its members so redeem his time, that he may receive the joyful invitation :· 'Enter thou into the joy of thy Lord.' Glory to God in the highest, and on earth peace, good will towards men."

Response.—"As it was in the beginning, is now, and ever shall be, world without end. Amen."

INSTALLATION.

The Eminent Commander elect is then presented to the Grand Commander by the Marshal, who says:

Right Eminent :—I have the honor to present you Eminent Sir ———, who has been elected to the office of Eminent Commander of this Commandery. I find him to be well skilled in our sublime mysteries, and observant of the noble precepts of our forefathers, and have, therefore, no doubt but he will discharge the important duties of his office with fidelity."

The Grand Commander then asks, "Eminent, are you ready to subscribe to the oath of office?" On his answering in the affirmative, the Grand Commander will draw his sword, and holding it horizontally, the edge toward the Eminent Commander elect, who will place his left hand on the same, and his right hand on his left breast, and repeat as follows:

"I, A. B., do solemnly promise, upon the honor of a Knight Templar, that I will, to the best of my knowledge and ability, faithfully discharge the various duties incumbent upon the office to which I have been elected, that I will support and maintain the By-Laws of this Commandery, and the laws and constitution of the Grand Commandery, under whose immediate authority I act; also the constitution and edicts of the Grand Encampment of the United States of America."

The Grand Commander will then address the Eminent Commander elect, as follows:

"EMINENT SIR:—Having been elected to the important and honorable station of Eminent Commander of this (new) Commandery, it is with unfeigned pleasure that I enter upon the discharge of the pleasing duty of installing you into your office. As the head of an institution founded upon the Christian religion, and the practice of the Christian virtues, you will sensibly realize the great responsibility of the new relation in which you now stand to your brethren; and, I am fully persuaded, will so conduct the important interests about to be committed to your hands, as to reflect honor upon yourself and credit upon your Commandery. It now, Sir Knight, becomes my duty to propose certain questions to you, relative to your office, to which I must request unequivocal answers.

I. Do you solemnly promise, upon the honor of a Knight Templar, that you will redouble your endeavors to correct the vices, purify the morals, and promote the happiness of those of your brethren who have attained this magnanimous Order?

II. That you will never suffer your Commandery to be opened, unless there be present seven regular Sir Knights of the Order?

III. That you will not confer the Orders upon any one who has not shown a charitable and humane disposition: or who has not made a considerable proficiency in the foregoing Degrees?

IV. That you will promote the general good of our Order, and on all proper occasions be ready to give and receive instructions, and particularly from the General and State Grand Officers?

V. That to the utmost of your power you will preserve the solemnities of our ceremonies, and behave, in open Commandery, with the most profound respect and reverence, as an example to your brethren?

VI. That you will not acknowledge or have intercourse with any Commandery that does not work under a constitutional Warrant or Dispensation?

VII. That you will not admit any visitor into your Commandery who has not been Knighted in a Commandery legally constituted, without his being first formally healed?

VIII. That you will pay due respect and obedience to the instructions of the general and State Grand officers, particularly relating to the several lectures and charges, and will resign the Chair to them severally, when they may visit your Commandery?

IX. That you will support and observe the Constitution of the Grand Encampment, and the General Regulations of the Grand Commandery under whose authority you act?

X. That you will bind your successor in office to the observance of the same rules to which you have now assented?

"Do you submit to all these things? and do you promise to observe and practice them faithfully?"
Assents.

CHARGE TO THE EMINENT COMMANDER.

 EMINENT:—You will now permit me to invest you with this badge of your office; It is a CROSS, surmounted by *Rays of Light*. It is an appropriate and beautiful emblem of the sublime principles of this magnanimous and Christian Order of Knighthood. The Cross will remind you of Him who offered up his life as a propitiation for the sins of the world; and the refulgent rays that emanate from it, of those divine teachings and sublime precepts which He

has left to guide and direct us in the paths of truth and holiness.

I present you the CHARTER of your Commandery. You will receive it as a sacred deposit, and never permit it to be used for any other purpose than those expressed in it, and safely transmit it to your successor in office.

I also commit to your hands the HOLY BIBLE, the Great Light in every degree of Masonry, together with the CROSS SWORDS. The doctrines contained in this sacred volume, create in us a belief in the existence of the eternal JEHOVAH, the one only true and living God, the Creator and Judge of all things in heaven and on earth. They also confirm in us a belief in the dispensations of his Providence. This belief strengthens our FAITH, and enables us to ascend the first step of the Grand Masonic Ladder. This FAITH naturally produces in us a HOPE of becoming partakers of the promises expressed in this inestimable gift of GOD to man, which hope enables us to ascend the second step. But the third and the last, being CHARITY, comprehends the former, and will continue to exert its influence when Faith shall be lost in sight, and Hope in complete enjoyment.

The CROSS SWORDS, resting upon the HOLY BIBLE, are to remind us that we should be "strong in the LORD, and in the power of his might;"—that we should "put on the whole armor of GOD," to be able to wrestle successfully against principalities and powers, and spiritual wickedness in high places.

I also present to you the Constitution of the Grand Encampment of the United States of America; the Rules and Regulations of the Grand Commandery of this State, and the By-laws of your Commandery. You will frequently consult them yourself, and cause them to be read for the information of your Commandery, that all, being informed of their duty, may have no reasonable excuse to offer for the neglect of it.

And now, Eminent Sir, permit me to induct you into the Chair of your Commandery, and, in behalf of the Sir Knights here assembled, to offer you my most sincere congratulations on your accession to the honorable station you now fill. It will henceforth be your special duty to preserve inviolate the Laws and Constitutions of the Order, to dispense justice, reward merit, encourage truth, and diffuse the sublime principles of universal benevolence. You will distribute alms to poor and weary pilgrims traveling from afar; feed the hungry; clothe the naked, and bind up the wounds of the afflicted. You will inculcate the duties of charity and hospitality, and govern your Commandery with justice and moderation. And finally, my brother, may the bright example of the illustrious heroes of former ages, whose matchless valor has shed undying luster over the name of Knight Templar, encourage and animate you to the faithful performance of every duty.

Sir Knights:—Behold your Eminent Commander, [*The Knights rise and present arms*]. Recollect, Sir

Knights, that the prosperity of your Commandery, will as much depend on your support, assistance and obedience, as on the assiduity, fidelity and wisdom of your Commander.

The remainder of the officers are then duly qualified, by taking the oath of office, in the form and manner before stated. The Grand Marshal then presents the Generalissimo.

CHARGE TO THE GENERALISSIMO.

SIR:—You have been elected Generalissimo of this Commandery. I now invest you with the badge of your office, which is a *Square*, surmounted by a *Paschal Lamb*. When beholding the lamb, let it stimulate you to have, at all times, a watchful eye over your own conduct, and an earnest solicitude for the prosperity of the kingdom of the blest Emmanuel, the spotless Lamb of God, who was slain from the foundation of the world.

The *square* is to remind you that the institution of Freemasonry, and the Orders of Knighthood were formerly governed by the same Grand Masters, and that the same principles of brotherly love and friendship should forever govern the members of both orders. Your station, Sir Knight, is on the right of your Commander; your duty is to receive and communicate all orders, signs and petitions: to assist your Commander in his various duties, and in his absence to preside in the Commandery. The exercise of all your talents and zeal will be necessary in the discharge of your various duties. I charge you, therefore, to be faithful to the Sir Knights with whom you are associated; put them often in remembrance of those things which tend to their everlasting peace. Finally, "preach to them the word: be instant in season, and out of season; reprove, rebuke, exhort with all long-suffering and doctrine;" ever remembering the promise, "Be thou faithful unto death, and I will give thee a crown of life."

CHARGE TO THE CAPTAIN-GENERAL.

 Sir:—You are elected Captain-General of this Commandery. I now invest you with the badge of your office, which is a *Level*, surmounted by a *Cock*. As the undaunted courage and valor of the cock stimulates him to conquer his competitor or yield himself a victim to the contest, so should you be stimulated to the discharge of every duty. You should have on "the breast-plate of righteousness," so that with patience and meekness you may ever travel on the *level* of humility, and be so supplied with divine grace as to prevent you from selling your God or denying your Master. Your station is on the left of your Commander. Your duty, among other things, is to see that the proper officers make all due preparation for the various meetings of the Commandery; that the council

chamber and asylum are in suitable array for the introduction of candidates and the dispatch of business. You are also to receive and communicate all orders issued by the Eminent Commander, through the officers of the line. You are to assist in Council, and in the absence of your Commander and Generalissimo, you are to govern the Commandery. The distressed widow, the helpless orphan, and the innocent of the weaker sex, you are ever to assist and protect. But, above all, you are to stand forth, having your loins girt about with TRUTH, in defense of the Christian religion from all its enemies. And now I exhort you, that with fidelity you perform every duty; and "Whatsoever ye do, do heartily as to the Lord, and not unto men: continue in prayer, and watch in the same with thanksgiving;" ever bearing in mind the promise, "Be not weary in well-doing, for in due time you shall reap if ye faint not."

CHARGE TO THE PRELATE.

 SIR:—You are elected Prelate of this Commandery. I have the pleasure of investing you with this *Triple Triangle*, which is the badge of your office, and a beautiful emblem of the Eternal Jehovah. Your station is on the right of the Generalissimo; your duty is to officiate at the *altar;* to offer up prayers and oblations to Deity. The duties of your office are very interesting

and highly important, and will require your early and punctual attendance at every meeting. Your jewel is to remind you of the importance of the trust reposed in you; and may " He who is able, abundantly furnish you for every good work, preserve you from falling into error; improve, strengthen, establish and perfect you," and, finally, greet you with, " Well done, good and faithful servant : enter thou into the joy of thy Lord."

CHARGE TO THE SENIOR WARDEN.

 SIR:—You are elected Senior Warden of this Commandery. I now invest you with the badge of your office, which is a *Hollow Square* and *Sword of Justice*. It is to remind you that as the children of Israel marched in a hollow square, in their journey through the wilderness, in order to guard and protect the *Ark* of the *Covenant*, so should you be vigilant in guarding every avenue from innovation and error. Let the sword of justice, therefore, be ever drawn to guard the Constitution of the Order. Your station is at the south-west angle of the triangle, and upon the right of the first division. You will attend *pilgrim warriors* traveling from afar, comfort and support *pilgrim penitents*, and recommend them, after due trial, to the favor and protection of the Eminent Commander. You will be assiduous in teaching your division their duties and exercises. You will, on all occasions, form the avenues for the approach and departure of your Commander; and prepare the lines for inspection and review. Let it be your constant care that the *warrior* be not deterred from duty, nor the *penitent* molested on his journey. Finally, "Let your light so shine before men, that they seeing your good works may glorify your Father which is in heaven."

CHARGE TO THE JUNIOR WARDEN.

SIR:—You are elected Junior Warden of this Commandery. I now invest you with the badge of your office, which is an *Eagle* and *Flaming Sword*. It is to remind you to perform your various duties with *justice* and *valor*, having an eagle eye on the prosperity of the Order. Your station is at the north-west angle of the triangle, and on the left of the third division. Your duty is to attend weary pilgrims, traveling from afar, conduct them on their journey, plead their cause, and, by permission of the Grand Commander, introduce them into the asylum. You will be careful that in addition to the *sandals*, *staff* and *scrip*, their whole preparation and deportment be such as shall cause them to be recognized as *children of humility*. Teach that "*Magna est veritas et prævalebit*" is the motto of our orders, and although in the course of their pilgrimage, they will often find the hights of fortune inaccessible, and the thorny path of life crooked, adverse and forlorn;

yet, by faith and humility, courage, constancy, and perseverance in the great duties set before them in the gospel, they may gain admission into the *asylum* above; there to enjoy the honor and rewards that await the *valiant soldiers* of the Lord Jesus Christ. Finally, be ye perfect, always abounding in the works of the Lord; that you may be a shining light in the world. A city that is set on a hill cannot be hid.

CHARGE TO THE TREASURER.

SIR:—You are elected Treasurer of this Commandery. I now invest you with the badge of your office. Your station is on the right of the Eminent Commander, in front. The qualities which should recommend a Treasurer are *accuracy* and *fidelity :* accuracy, in keeping a fair and minute account of all receipts and disbursements; fidelity, in carefully preserving all the property and funds of the Commandery, that may be placed in his hands, and rendering a just account of the same whenever he is called upon for that purpose. I presume that your respect and attachment to the Commandery, and your earnest solicitude for a good name, which is better than precious ointment, will prompt you to the faithful discharge of the duties of your office.

CHARGE TO THE RECORDER.

SIR:—You are elected Recorder of this Commandery. I now invest you with the badge of your office. Your station is on the left of the Eminent Commander, in front. The qualities which should recommend a Recorder are, *promptitude* in issuing the notifications and orders of his superior officers; *punctuality* in attending the meetings of the Commandery; *correctness* in recording their proceedings; *judgment* in discriminating between what is proper and what is improper to be committed to writing; *integrity* in accounting for all moneys that may pass through his hands, and *fidelity* in paying the same over into the hands of the Treasurer. The possession of these good qualities, I presume, has designated you as a suitable candidate for this important office; and I cannot entertain a doubt that you will discharge its duties beneficially to the Commandery and honorably to yourself. And when you shall have completed the record of your transactions here below, and finished the term of your probation, may you be admitted into the celestial *asylum* of saints and angels, and find your name *recorded in the* LAMB'S *Book of Life.*

CHARGE TO THE STANDARD BEARER.

Sir:—You are elected Standard Bearer of this Commandery. I now invest you with the badge of your office, which is a *Plumb* surmounted by a *Banner*. Your station is in the west, and in the centre of the second division. Your duty is to display, support and protect the standard of the Order, which I now, with pleasure, confide to your valor. You will remember that it is our rallying point in time of danger; and, when unfurled in a just and virtuous cause, you will never relinquish it to an enemy but with your life. Let, therefore, your conduct be such as all the virtuous will delight to imitate; let the refulgent rays which ever emanate from pure *benevolence* and *humility*, diffuse their luster on all around, that it may encourage and animate all true and courteous knights, and, at the same time, confound and dismay all their enemies.

CHARGE TO THE SWORD BEARER.

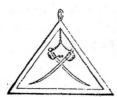

Sir:—You are elected Sword Bearer of this Commandery. I now invest you with the badge of your office, which is a *Triangle* and *Cross Swords*. Your station is on the right of the Standard Bearer, and on the right of the second division, when formed in line. Your duty is to watch all orders and signals from the Eminent Commander, and see that they are promptly obeyed. You are also to assist in the protection of the banners of the Order, and with a heart lively devoted to the principles of *Faith*, *Hope* and *Charity*; with the mystic sword that is endowed with *justice* and *fortitude*, and tempered by *mercy*, in your hand, you may cast your eyes upon the standard, and remember that "*In hoc signo vinces*" is an expressive motto of our Order, and consoling to the heart of every believer.

CHARGE TO THE WARDER.

SIR:—You are elected Warder of this Commandery. I now invest you with the badge of your office, which is a *Square Plate*, with a *Trumpet* and *Cross Swords* engraved thereon. Your station is upon the left of the Standard Bearer, and upon the left of the second division, when formed in line. Your duty is to announce the approach and departure of the Eminent Commander; to post the sentinels, and see that the asylum is duly guarded. You will, also, report all petitions from visitors and strangers, and communicate the orders of your superior officers; and I charge you to be punctual in your attendance at our meetings, and indefatigable in the discharge of your important duties; for though yours is among the last offices in the Commandery, it is by no means the least in importance.

19

CHARGE TO THE THREE GUARDS.

 SIR KNIGHTS:—You are appointed Captains of the Guards. I now invest you with your badge of office, which is a *Square Plate*, with a *Battle Ax* engraved thereon. Your post is that of honor as well as danger. You will therefore be vigilant, and challenge with spirit, *examine* with caution, *admonish* with candor, *relieve* cheerfully, *protect* with fidelity, and *fight* valiantly.

CHARGE TO THE COMMANDERY.

SIR KNIGHTS :—To manage and conduct the concerns of a Commandery of Knights Templar with that promptitude, integrity and skill which the institution demands, will require the exercise of all the talents, and perseverance of its officers and members. Are any of you solicitous that your equals and inferiors should conduct themselves toward you with deference and respect ? you will be sure to let no opportunity pass without furnishing them an example in your own conduct toward your superiors. The officers will recollect that those moral and religious duties and precepts which they, from time to time, so forcibly impress upon the minds of others, should by no means be neglected by themselves ; as the most effectual way to insure success, is to let precept and example go hand in hand.

I would therefore exhort one and all of you to look well to the East, to the West, to the North and to the

South, and see that the *entering avenues* are strictly guarded, and that you suffer no one to pass the threshold of your asylum but the worthy *children* of *humility*, and, at the same time, that you suffer no one to walk among you disorderly without admonition or reproof. While such is the conduct of the officers and members, you may rest assured that this valiant magnanimous order will forever flourish like the *green bay tree.* And now, my worthy Sir Knights, I would address you in the language of David to his beloved city, "Peace be within thy walls, and prosperity within thy palaces." For my brethren and companions' sake, I will now say, *Peace be with thee.*

The Grand Marshal then proclaims the new Commandery in the following manner, viz.:

" In the name of the Most Eminent Grand Commandery of the State of ———, I proclaim this new Commandery, by the name of ——— Commandery, to be legally constituted, consecrated, and the officers duly installed."

After the necessary business is finished the Commandery is closed.

ODE.

Music—"Sweet Home."

Farewell, till again we shall welcome the time
Which brings us once more to our fame-cherished
    shrine ;
And though from each other we distant may roam,
Again may all meet in this our dear lov'd home
    Home, home—sweet, sweet home.
May every dear brother find joy and peace at home.

And when our last parting on earth shall draw nigh,
And we shall be called to the Grand Lodge on high,
May each be prepared when the summons shall
    come,
To meet the Grand Master in Heaven our home
    Home, home—sweet, sweet home.
May every dear brother find Heaven a home

———

INSTALLATION ODE

Music—"Rule Britannia."

When earth's foundation first was laid,
  By the Almighty Artist's hand ;
'Twas then our perfect. our perfect laws were made,
  Established by his strict command.

    Hail! mysterious, Hail, glorious Masonry !
    That makes us ever great and free

In vain mankind for shelter sought,
  In vain from place to place did roam,
Until from heaven, from heaven he was taught
  To plan, to build, to fix his home.

Illustrious hence we date our Art,
  And now in beauteous piles appear,
We shall to endless, to endless time impart,
✦ How worthy and how great we are.

Nor we less fam'd for every tie,
  By which the human thought is bound ;
Love, truth and *friendship*, and friendship socially,
  Join all our hearts and hands around.

Our actions still by Virtue blest,
  And to our precepts ever true,
The world admiring, admiring shall request
  To learn, and our bright paths pursue.

————

ON CONSECRATION OF A LODGE

Music—" God save the King."

  Hail, Masonry divine !
  Glory of ages, shine !
  Long may'st thou reign :
  Where'er thy Lodges stand,
  May they have great command,
  And always grace the land.
    Thou art divine !

Great fabrics still arise,
And grace the azure skies ;
Great are thy schemes ;
Thy noble orders are
Matchless, beyond compare ;
No art with thee can share.
    Thou art divine !

Hiram, the architect,
Did all the Craft direct
How they should build.
Sol'mon, great Israel's king, ⎫
Did mighty blessings bring,   ⎬ Chorus,
And left us room to sing,   ⎭ 3 times
    Hail, royal art !

DEDICATION OF MASONIC HALL.

MUSIC—Old Hundred, L. M.

Great Architect of Heaven and earth,
To whom all nature owes its birth ;
Thou spake ! and vast creation stood,
Surveyed the work—pronounced it good.

Lord, can'st thou deign to own and bless
This humble dome—this sacred place ?
Oh ! let thy Spirit's presence shine
Within these walls—this house of thine.

'T was reared in honor of thy name.
Here kindle, Lord, the sacred flame ;
Oh! make it burn in every heart,
And never from this place depart

Here may our precepts' powerful truth,
Instruct the aged and the youth ;
Nor let illiberal party zeal,
E'er mar the union, Masons feel.

Let life divine here seize the dead ;
Here may the starving poor be fed ;
Here may the mourner comfort find ;
Here love prevail for all mankind.

Lord, here the wants of all supply,
And fit our souls to dwell on high ;
From service in this humble place,
Raise us to praise thee face to face

ODE AT LAYING A CORNER STONE.

AIR—Creation.

Deep in the quarries of the stone,
  Amid vast heaps of other rock ,
In darkness hid, to art unknown,
  We found this rude and shapeless block.
Now shaped by art, its roughness gone,
  And fit this noble work to grace ;
And lay it here, a corner stone,
  Chosen and sure, in proper place

Within this stone there lies conceal'd
  What future ages may disclose,
The sacred truths to us reveal'd,
  By Him who fell by ruthless foes.
On Him, this corner stone we build,
  To Him, this edifice erect ;
And still, until this work's fulfill'd,
  May Heaven the workman's ways direct

ROYAL ARCH SONG

Music—"Safely through another week."

Joy ! the sacred Law is found,
  Now the Temple stands complete ;
Gladly let us gather round,
  Where the Pontiff holds his seat
Now he spreads the volume wide,
  Opening forth its leaves to day,
And the monarch by his side,
  Gazes on the bright display.

Joy ! the secret vault is found ;
  Full the sunbeam falls within,
Pointing darkly under ground.
  To the treasure we would win.
They have brought it forth to light,
  And again it cheers the earth ;
All its leaves are purely bright,
  Shining in their newest worth

This shall be the sacred mark,
Which shall guide us to the skies,
Bearing, like a holy ark,
All the hearts who love to rise ;
This shall be the corner stone
Which the builders threw away,
But was found the only one
Fitted for the arch's stay.

ROYAL ARCH CLOSING.

Music—Shirland.

Companions we have met,
    And passed a peaceful hour ;
These moments may we ne'er forget,
    But hope and pray for more.

Thro' this and every night,
    Lord, grant us sweet repose ;
Now aid us by thy holy light,
    This Royal Arch to close.

TEMPLAR'S SONG

As, when the weary trav'ler gains
    The height of some commanding hill,
His heart revives, if o'er the plains
    He sees his home, though distant still

So, when the Christian pilgrim views
    By faith his mansion in the skies,
The sight his fainting strength renews,
    And wings his speed to reach the prize.

The hope of heaven his spirit cheers;
    No more he grieves for sorrows past;
Nor any future conflict fears,
    So he may safe arrive at last.

O Lord, on thee our hopes we stay,
    To lead us on to thine abode;
Assur'd thy love will far o'erpay
    The hardest labors of the road

THE MASON'S ADIEU

Words by BURNS.   AIR—Bonny Doon.

ADIEU, a heart warm, fond adieu,
    Ye brothers of our mystic tie;
Ye favored and enlighten'd few,
    Companions of my social joy;
Though I to foreign lands must hie,
    Pursuing fortune's slipp'ry ba';
With melting heart and brimful eye,
    I'll mind you still when far awa'

Oft have I met your social band,
    To spend a cheerful festive night,
Oft honor'd with supreme command,
    Presiding o'er the sons of light:

And by that hieroglyphic bright,
 Which none but craftsmen ever saw,
Strong mem'ry on my heart shall write,
 Those happy scenes when far awa'.

May freedom, harmony and love,
 Cement you in the grand design,
Beneath th' Omniscient Eye above,
 The glorious Architect divine:
That you may keep th' unerring line,
 Still guided by the plummet's law,
'Till order bright completely shine,
 Shall be my prayer when far awa'

And you, farewell, whose merits claim
 Justly that highest badge to wear,
May heaven bless your noble name,
 To Masonry and friendship dear :
My last request permit me then,
 When yearly you're assembled a ,
One round, I ask it with a tear,
 To him, your friend that's far awa'

And you, kind-hearted sisters, fair,
 I sing farewell to all your charms—
Th' impression of your pleasing air
 With rapture oft my bosom warms,
Alas ! the social winter's night
 No more returns while breath I draw
'Till sisters, brothers, all unite,
 In that Grand Lodge that's far awa'

MASONIC CALENDAR.

In affixing dates to official Masonic documents, Freemasons should always use the calendar peculiar to themselves: the common calendar, or vulgar era, may also be used in tl e same instrument. The dates vary in the different branches of the order.

Masons of the York and French rites, date from the creation of th world, calling it "Anno Lucis," which they abbreviate A∴ L∴ signifying "in the year of Light." Thus with them the present year is A∴ L∴ 5852. Masons of the York rite begin the year on the first of January, but in the French rite it commences on the first of March, and instead of the months receiving their usual names, they are designated numerically, as first, second, third, &c. Thus, the 1st of January, 1852, would be styled, in a French Masonic document, the "1st day of the 11th Masonic month. Anno Lucis, 5852." The French, sometimes, instead of the initials A∴ L∴, use "L'an de la V∴ L∴, or "Vraie Lumiere," that is "Year of True Light."

Royal Arch Masons commence their era with the year in which Zerubbabel began to build the second temple, which was 530 years before Christ. Their style for the year 1852 is, therefore, A∴ Inv∴, that is, Anno Inventionis, or, in the year of the Discovery, 2382.

Royal and Select Masters very often make use of the common masonic date, Anno Lucis, but properly they should date from the year in which Solomon's Temple was completed; and their style would then be, Anno Depositionis, or, in the Year of the Deposit, and they would date the present year as 2852.

Knights Templars use the era of the organization of their order, in 1118. Their style for the present year is A∴ O∴, Anno Ordinis, or, in the year of the Order, 734.

Rules for discovering the different Dates.

1. To FIND THE ANCIENT CRAFT. Add 4000 to the vulgar era. Thus 1852 and 4000 are 5852.

2. To FIND THE DATE OF ROYAL ARCH MASONRY. Add 530 to the vulgar era. Thus 530 and 1852 are 2382.

3. To FIND THE ROYAL AND SELECT MASTER'S DATE. Add 1000 ● the vulgar era. Thus 1000 and 1852 are 2852.

4. To FIND THE KNIGHTS TEMPLARS' DATE. Subtract 1118 from the vulgar era. Thus 1118 from 1852 is 734.

The following table shows, in one view, the date of the present year in all the branches of the Order:

Year of the Lord, A. D.	1852—Vulgar era.
Year of the Light, A∴ L∴	5852—Ancient Craft Masonry.
Year of the Discovery, A∴ I∴	2382—Royal Arch Masonry.
Year of the Deposit, A∴ Dep∴	2852—Royal and Select Masters.
Year of the Order, A∴ O∴	734—Knights Templars.

FORMS OF MASONIC DOCUMENTS.

[For the form of petition to constitute a new Lodge, see Present, or Past Master's degree, p. 98.]

DISPENSATION FOR CONSTITUTING A NEW LODGE.

To all whom it may concern :

KNOW YE, That we, Q— R—, Most Worshipful Grand Master of Ancient, Free and Accepted Masons of ——, having received a petition from a constitutional number of brethren, who have been properly vouched for as Master Masons in good standing, setting forth, that having the honor and prosperity of the Craft at heart, they are desirous of establishing a new Lodge at —— under our masonic jurisdiction, and requesting a Dispensation for the same : And whereas there appears to us, good and sufficient cause for granting the prayer of the said petition ; we, by virtue of the powers in us vested by the ancient Constitutions of the Order, do grant this our DISPENSATION, empowering Brother A— B —, to act as Worshipful Master, Brother C— D—, to act as Senior Warden, and Brother E— F, to act as Junior Warden of a Lodge to be held under our jurisdiction at * * * * * by the name of ——. And we further authorize the said brethren, to *Enter*, *Pass* and *Raise* Free-masons, according to the Ancient Constitutions of the Order, the customs and usages of the Craft, and the Rules and Regulations of the Most Worshipful Grand Lodge of * * * * * *shall continue of erwise. And this our DISPENS aforesaid shall grant a force until the Grand Lodge for the same, or this Dispensation be revoked by us, or the authority of the aforesaid Grand Lodge. Given under our hand, and the seal of the Grand Lodge, at —— this —— day of ——, A∴ L∴ 58 .

[L. S.]

Q— R—,
Grand Master

Y— Z—,
Grand Secretary

CERTIFICATE OF SUBORDINATE LODGE

To all enlightened and Accepted Ancient Free-masons
throughout the globe, GREETING:

KNOW YE, That the bearer. hereof Brother J — K,
has been regularly initiated as an ENTERED APPREN-
TICE, passed as a FELLOW CRAFT and raised to the Sublime Degree of a MASTER MASON; and having worked
among us to our entire satisfaction. as a true. faithful and worthy brother, WE. the Worshipful Master,
Wardens and Brethren of ———— Lodge, No. —, recommend that he be received and acknowledged as such,
by all true and accepted Ancient Free-masons where-
soever dispersed.

In testimony whereof, we have granted him
this certificate. under the seal of our
Lodge, first causing him to write his
name in the margin, that he alone may
have the benefit thereof.

Given at——, this—— day of——,
in the year of light, 58—.

A—— B——, *Worshipful Master.*

[L. S.]   C—— D——, *Senior Warden.*

E—— F——, *Junior Warden.*

G—— H——, *Secretary.*

Grand Lodge of————.

This is to certify. that ———— Lodge. No. —, is a
legally constituted Lodge, working under the jurisdiction of the Grand Lodge of ————, and that this di-
brethren. therefore entitled to full credit among the

Y—— Z——, *Grand Secretary.*

WARRANT OF CONSTITUTION.

(FOR A SUBORDINATE LODGE.)

To all whom it may concern:

The most Worshipful Grand Lodge of ————, assembled in Grand Communication in the city of ——, and
State of ——, SEND GREETING:

KNOW YE. That we, the Grand Lodge of ——, invested with full power and authority over all the Craft,
and Supreme Court of Appeal in all Masonic cases

arising under its jurisdiction, do hereby authorize and empower our trusty and well-beloved brethren, A— B—, Worshipful Master ; C— D—, as Senior Warden, and E— F—, Junior Warden ; to open and hold a Lodge by the name of ———, to be designated in our register as number —; the said Lodge to be holden at——, or within three miles of the same.

And we do likewise authorize and empower our said brethren, A— B—, C— D—, and E— F, to *Enter, Pass* and *Raise* Free-masons, according to the most ancient custom and usage of the Craft, in all ages and nations throughout the world, and not otherwise.

And we do further authorize and empower the said A— B, C— D, and E— F—, and their successors in office, to hear all and singular, matters and things, relative to the Craft within the jurisdiction of the said Lodge.

And lastly, we do further authorize, empower and direct our said trusty and well-beloved brethren, A— B—, C— D—, and E—F—, to install their successors in office, after being elected and chosen ; to invest them with all the powers and dignities to their offices respectively belonging, and to deliver to them this War-rant of Constitution : and such successors shall, in like manner, from time to time, install their successors, and proceed in the premises as above directed : Such installation to be upon, or immediately preceding the Festival of St. John the Evangelist, during the continuance of the said Lodge forever. Provided, always, That the above named brethren, and their successors do pay, and cause to be paid, due respect and obedience to the Most Worshipful Grand Lodge of ———, aforesaid, and to the by-laws, rules, regulations and edicts thereof ; otherwise, this Warrant of Constitution to be of no force nor virtue.

Given in open Grand Lodge, under the hands of our Grand Officers, and the seal of our Grand Lodge, at ——, this—— day of ——, Anno Domini, 18--, and Anno Lucis, 58--.

Q—— R——,   W—— V——,
 Grand Master.   *Senior Grand Warden.*

S—— T——,   W—— X——,
 Deputy Grand Master [L. S.] *Junior Grand Warden*

  Y—— Z——, *Grand Secretary.*

EMPOWERING A PAST MASTER TO CONSTITUTE A NEW LODGE, AND INSTALL ITS OFFICERS ELECT.

To all whom it may concern :

But more especially, to Brothers A— B—, Worshipful Master elect ; C— D, Senior Warden elect ; and E— F—, Junior Warden elect, and the rest of the brethren who have been empowered by Warrant of Constitution regularly issued under the authority of the Most Worshipful Grand Lodge of ——, to assemble as a regular Lodge in the town of ——.

KNOW YE, That reposing special trust and confidence in the skill, prudence and integrity of our W Brother L— M—, we have thought proper, ourselves being unable to attend, to nominate and appoint our said Worshipful Brother L— M—, to constitute "IN FORM," the brethren aforesaid, into a regular Lodge, to be known and distinguished by the name of —— Lodge, No.—, and to instal their officers elect, according to ancient form and the usages of the Craft ; and for so doing, this shall be his Warrant.

Given under our hand and the seal of
[L. S.]   the Grand Lodge, at ——, this —— day of ——, A∴ L∴, 58—.

Q—— R——,
Grand Master.

Y—— Z —,
Grand Secretary.

APPOINTMENT OF PROXY TO REPRESENT A LODGE IN THE GRAND LODGE.

To the Most Worshipful Grand Lodge of ——.

In consideration of the confidence we repose in the skill and integrity of our Worshipful Brother S—— T——, we have nominated and appointed, and by these presents do nominate and appoint our said Worshipful Brother S—— T——, to be our proxy in the Grand Lodge, and there to represent us and to do every act and thing agreeably to the Constitutions of the Order, and the rules and regulations of the Grand Lodge, as fully and completely as the officers of our Lodge could do were they personally present

Witness the hands of our Worshipful Master
[L. S.]   and Secretary, and the seal of the Lodge,
at —, this — day of —, A∴ L∴ 58—.

A—— B——, *W. Master*

B—— C——, *Secretary.*

ROYAL ARCH CERTIFICATE

HOLINESS TO THE LORD.

To all the Enlightened, Entered, Passed, Raised and
Exalted under the canopy of Heaven :

Wr., the undersigned, officers of the Grand Royal
Chapter of ——, Do certify, that the bearer, our truly
beloved Companion, A— B—, who hath, in the margin
hereof, signed his name, has been regularly admitted
to the degree of Mark Master, inducted into the Oriental chair of King Solomon, and received and
acknowledged as a Most Excellent Master;
and that having sustained with fortitude, the
severe trials required from all, previous to
their admission into our Order, he has been
exalted to the august degree of a ROYAL ARCH
MASON. As such, we recommend him to all
our dear and Excellent Companions throughout the two hemispheres, and enjoin it on them to
recognize him.

Given under the hands and seal of the Grand
Chapter at —, this— day of —, A. D., 18—,
and in the year of the Discovery 23—.

G——H——, *G. H. Priest.* [L. S.] L——M——, *G. King.*
J——K——, *Dep. G. H. P.*   N——O——, *G. Scribe.*
R—— S——, *Grand Secretary.*

Grand Chapter of ——.

This is to certify, that —— Chapter, No. —, is a
legally constituted Chapter, working under the jurisdiction of the Grand Chapter of ——, and that this
diploma is therefore entitled to full credit among the
Companions.

Y—— Z——, *Grand Secretary.*

KNIGHT TEMPLARS' DIPLOMA.

IN HOC SIGNO VINCES.

To all Sir Knights of the Illustrious Order of the Red Cross, and of the Valiant and Magnanimous Orders of Knights Templars and Knights of Malta, around the globe, to whom these presents may come, GREETING :

WE, the presiding officers of ———— Encampment, of Knights Templars, No.—, held at ————, do certify and make known, that our Illustrious Sir Knight L—— M·——, having previously received the necessary degrees. has been regularly dubbed and created in this Encampment, a Knight of the Illustrious Order of the Red Cross, and of the Valiant and Magnanimous Order of Knights Templars, and Knights of Malta, or Order of St. John of Jerusalem. We do, therefore, cordially recommend him to the friendship, assistance and protection of all Valiant and Magnanimous Sir Knights in all parts of the globe, wherever he may go.

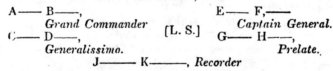

In testimony whereof, having first caused our Illustrious Sir Knight to sign his name in the margin, we have hereunto set our hands, and caused the seal of our Encampment to be affixed this —— day of ————, in the year of the Lord, 1850, and of the Order, 733.

A—— B——,   E—— F,——
Grand Commander   [L. S.]   *Captain General.*
C—— D——,   G—— H——,
Generalissimo.   *Prelate.*
J———— K————, *Recorder*

Grand Encampment of ————.

This is to certify, that —— Encampment, No. —, is a legally constituted Encampment, working under the jurisdiction of the Grand Encampment of ————, and that this diploma is therefore entitled to full credit among the Sir Knights.

Y—— Z——, *Grand Recorder*

SUBORDINATE LODGE JEWELS.

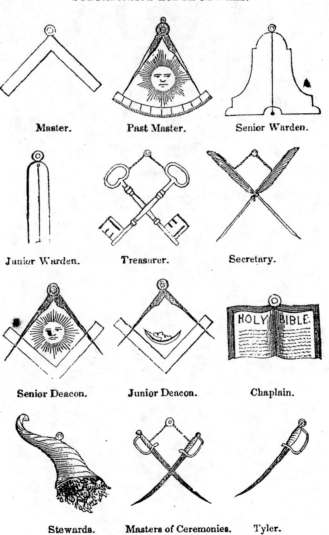

Master.   Past Master.   Senior Warden.

Junior Warden.   Treasurer.   Secretary.

Senior Deacon.   Junior Deacon.   Chaplain.

Stewards.   Masters of Ceremonies.   Tyler.

GRAND LODGE JEWELS.

Grand Master.

P. G. Master.

D. G. Master.

S. G. Warden.

J. G. Warden.

Grand Secretary.

Grand Treasurer.

Grand Chaplain.

Grand Marshal.

G. Stand. Bearer.

G. Sword Bearer.

Grand Stewards.

Grand Deacons.

G. Pursuivant.

Grand Tyler.

GRAND LODGE JEWELS—(California.)

GRAND LODGE JEWELS.—(ENGLISH.)

1. Collar and Jewel of the G. M.; 2. D. G. M.; 3. S.G.W.; 4. P.D.G.M.;
5. G.Chap.; 6. J.G.W.; 7. G. Regist.; 8. G. Sec.; 9. G. Treas.; 10. G. Dea

Grand and Subordinate Lodge Jewels.—(English.)

1. G. Sup. of Works; 2. G. Director of Cer.; 3. G. S. B.; 4. G. Organist;
G. Purs.; 6. G. Steward; 7. G. Tyler; 8. Collar of P. G. Officer; 9.
o. G. M.; 10. Master of Lodge; 11. D. Pro. G. M.: 12. P. Master; 13.
ner Guardian; 14. Tyler.

ROYAL ARCH JEWELS.

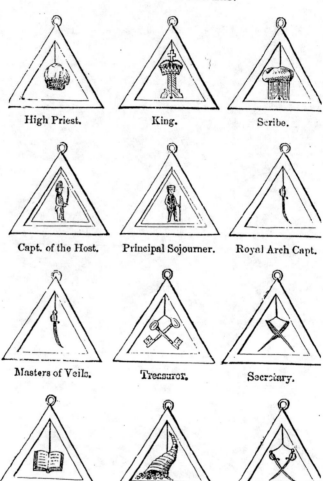

High Priest.

King.

Scribe.

Capt. of the Host.

Principal Sojourner.

Royal Arch Capt.

Masters of Veils.

Treasurer.

Secretary.

Chaplain.

Stewards.

Sentinel.

ENCAMPMENT JEWELS.

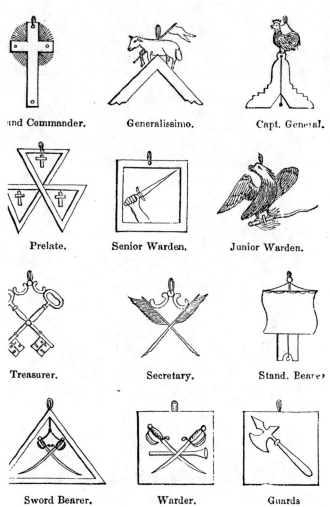

and Commander.   Generalissimo.   Capt. General.

Prelate.   Senior Warden.   Junior Warden.

Treasurer.   Secretary.   Stand. Bearer

Sword Bearer.   Warder.   Guards

ROYAL ARCH JEWELS—(English.)

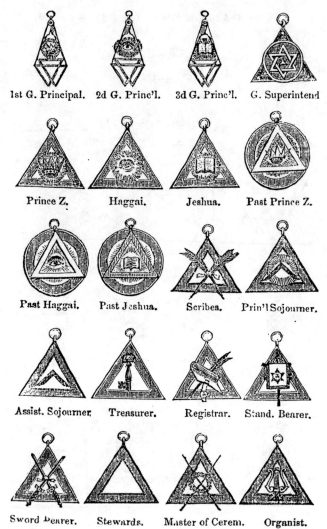

1st G. Principal.	2d G. Princ'l.	3d G. Princ'l.	G. Superintend
Prince Z.	Haggai.	Jeshua.	Past Prince Z.
Past Haggai.	Past Jeshua.	Scribes.	Prin'l Sojourner.
Assist. Sojourner	Treasurer.	Registrar.	Stand. Bearer.
Sword Bearer.	Stewards.	Master of Cerem.	Organist.

ROYAL ARCH JEWEL AND COLLAR—(English.)

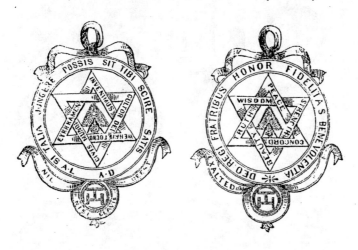

GRAND ROYAL ARCH CHAPTER JEWELS.

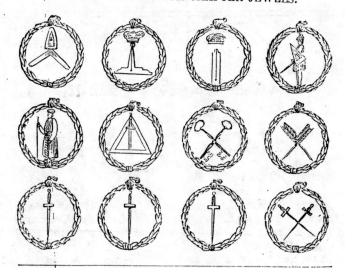

GRAND ENCAMPMENT JEWELS.